"As a wife, mother of three an method contains all the pr contributed significantly to n women." —Carolyn C.

"Gimme Five! will give you ten times more than any other self-help book. Josie Melo has walked the walk and she generously gives you the secrets of success in a system that explains what you need to do and how to do it." —Susan RoAne, keynote speaker and author of How to Work A Room

" 'Find someone who has what you want and do as they do to get the same results.' I did! Josie leads by example so everything she trains on she has done and proven. You walk away with a game plan and the tools to achieve it." —Jamie Cabrerra, Entrepreneur

"In Gimme Five!, *Josie Melo has been given a special gift in understanding the keys to prosperity. As a visionary her leadership and example pressed me to new levels of confidence and success. She deserves praise for presenting a book that explodes with penetrating insight and wisdom that leads to a triumphant life! Her step-by-step roadmap promotes the confidence to adapt to change and the fundamentals to master lasting success. Full of energy and ambition Josie has assembled a refreshing, powerful and informative tool for anyone committed to enriching the quality of their life.*

"Through Josie's Gimme Five! Method, her friendship and mentoring I have developed the heart and mind of a Champion and am living a fulfilled life and continuing to pursue dreams once dormant."
—Dana LeBlanc Corvino

"Few books can truly be defined as life-changing but Gimme Five! *by Josie Melo certainly deserves the term. In a clear, practical fashion, interspersed with real-life examples, Josie takes the reader by the hand and demonstrates exactly how to realize your dreams. Every young woman about to leave home, should be given a copy of* Gimme Five! *Every woman facing divorce, unemployment, the loss of a spouse, or in any situation that is short of the life she longs for, should read this book.* Gimme Five! *is a life-changing tool."*
—Claire Starr, author of What Saved Me: A Dozen Ways to Embrace Life

Gimme Five!

Increase Your Income, Enrich Your Life
and*
Have Fun Doing It
(*best of all!)

Josie Melo

Bamboo Press, Inc.

Bamboo Press, Inc.
809-B Cuesta Drive #154
Mountain View, California 94040

ISBN: 0-9747408-0-2
Library of Congress Control Number: 2003115210

Book design by Janice M. Phelps

Printed in the United States of America

First Edition

This book is dedicated to a very special man, my husband Joe, whose love and support are infinite and to our beautiful children Jason and Jackie, the greatest joy in life.

A Special Thanks

A special thanks to Toni Boyle whose collaboration on this book has made this dream a reality. She encouraged me and supported me throughout the entire process. Toni's confidence in my ability, her professional expertise, contacts in the industry and direction in the material and content has made *Gimme Five!* a book I'm so very proud of. More importantly, her friendship, support, and wisdom throughout this process have given me another opportunity to grow and learn as a professional, mother, and friend.

Janice Phelps is a creative, gifted and talented artist who captured the essence of the *Gimme Five!* Method and graphically display it in the book cover design. Her guidance and experience as a writer, editor and publisher made this a journey I will always treasure. Her patience and professionalism in guiding me through the publishing process will be forever appreciated.

To all the people I have had the opportunity to meet, learn from and train, thank you for the gift of your success. The greatest pleasure in working with you and knowing you has been the experience of seeing you grow professionally, financially and personally. May you always be blessed with life's abundance and surrounded by love.

Why Should You Buy this Book?

You need to buy this book if:

- You're in a transition in your life — or contemplating one.
- You're working for a company that provides you with good benefits and the promise of a secure retirement...
- You're 20 through 60 years old or older and haven't planned for your retirement...
- You're a single mother who needs additional income...
- You're a working mother who wants to stay home with your children without your husband working two or three jobs...
- You're not making enough money and can't figure out if or how you ever will...
- You're unhappy with your life and don't know how to fix it...
- You have a goal and don't think you'll ever attain it.

The Gallup Poll reports that in 2003 nearly one-third of Americans (32%) worry about not having enough money to pay their normal monthly bills. That figure is higher for single women and minorities.

In the April 15, 2003 issue, *Family Circle* magazine reported on their national survey of 3,315 men and women. Based on reader responses in January, 2003, 64% of Americans say they are living paycheck to paycheck, including 49% of those with yearly incomes from $50,000–$99,999. More amazing, 24% of those with incomes of $100,000 or more are in the same situation. If just one spouse lost their job, the couple would have to file for bankruptcy within three months.

Then there's retirement. To get the shocking facts on where most Americans are on the day they retire, look at the Thought Provoker on page xi.

This book will give you the information, skills and confidence to turn your life around. Whether you want more money or to break old habits or to enrich your life, the *Gimme Five!* Method will show you how to set goals, learn new skills, and become money-smart, people-smart and options-smart so you're able to achieve your goals. It's a no-nonsense roadmap to a better life - put together by someone who has not only done it herself, but has taught thousands of other to do it, too.

And here's another reason to buy this book...even if your life is perfect, I'll bet you know someone else you can give it to who really needs it.

Thought Provoker:
Is This Your Future?

Many of us wait eagerly for the day we can retire and do whatever we want. Well, before you quit your job and sign up for social security, you'd better look at these stunning facts.

Statistics show that of every 100 people age 65:
- 56 depend on the government for financial support;
- 34 will die within the year;
- 5 are still working, unable to retire;
- 4 are financially comfortable;
- 1 is rich.

Perhaps our parents and grandparents could depend on the pension awarded them by grateful companies, but today countless thousands of Americans watch their retirement money go up in corporate smoke. Every year the future availability of social security funds becomes less sure. The sad fact is that 55% of the working population have never attempted to plan for their retirement. The point is, you have one person in this world you can depend on for your security — and that person is you!

Here are some more frightening facts.

More than 40% of women ages 25–55 fear living at or near the poverty level during their retirement years. Many would like to retire before age 60, but don't expect they will be able to until at least age 70. Of those polled, half plan to support themselves by taking full-time or part-time jobs after reaching retirement age. Sixty percent of African-American and 57% of Hispanic women report they will have to work *after* reaching retirement age.*

Here's a sample of what the U.S. government considers the poverty level in 2003: $8,980 for a single person, $12,120 for a family of two, and $18,400 for a family of four.

Try and live on that! Worse news, only 23% of households below the poverty level receive government cash assistance.**

* *(1999 National Women's Retirement Survey by Heinz Foundation and Sun-America)*

** *(Poverty in the United States: 2002 Annual Demographic Supplement to the Current Population Survey)*

Table of Contents

Introduction xv

Section I: BECOME SELF-SMART

Gimme Five! Rule Number One:
"Know who you are."

Chapter 1:   Your Past Doesn't Equal Your Future 3
Chapter 2:   What Do You Consider Success? Happiness? 11
Chapter 3:   How to Set a Course and Follow It...........................15
                Thought Provoker: Tomorrow is Too Late........................20
Chapter 4:   Building Your Belief and Taking a Leap of Faith.........21
Chapter 5:   The Secret to Getting Focused and
                Staying Motivated...28

Section II: BECOME VISION- AND GOAL-SMART

Gimme Five! Rule Number Two:
"You will be who you believe you will be . . ."

Chapter 6:   See and Say Your Dream into Reality.........................35
Chapter 7:   "Soon," "Someday" and "Eventually"
                Aren't on the Calendar.......................................40
Chapter 8:   Signs along the Road to Success...............................44
Chapter 9:   Uncover Your Brilliance 51
Chapter 10:   Ask and the Universe Will Answer..............................61
                Thought Provoker: Check Your Attitude..........................72

Section III: BECOME MONEY-SMART

Gimme Five! Rule Number Three:
"Use money as a tool and not as a prize, and it will build you a fortune."

Chapter 11:   The Time and Money Relationship 75
Chapter 12:   Solving the Money Mystery 82
Chapter 13:   Abundance in Money and More 87
                Thought Provoker: The Power of Doubling......................92
Chapter 14:   Start with Business Basics 93
Chapter 15:   Make Money, Save Money, Grow Your Money.........101

Section IV: BECOME PEOPLE-SMART

Gimme Five! Rule Number Four:
"The More You Understand People, the More Successful You Will Be."

Chapter 16:   The Power of a Championship Circle 117
Chapter 17:   People Skills for Life 128
Chapter 18:   The Personality Rainbow 132
                *Thought Provoker: They Said It Couldn't
                Be Done* *142*
Chapter 19:   Do It Anyway 143
                *Thought Provoker:
                They Said It Wouldn't Work* *149*
Chapter 20:   Mentoring Magic 150

Section V: BECOME OPTIONS-SMART

Gimme Five! Rule Number Five:
"You have only one option – the option to do something now."

Chapter 21:   Quitting Is Not an Option 161
                Thought Provoker: Don't Quit *166*
Chapter 22:   Pick Your Pathway to Success....................................167
Chapter 23:   Stay on Track While Keeping Your Balance 184
Chapter 24:   Every Plan Has an Exit Strategy................................193
Chapter 25:   A Time to Review 201

Note from Josie 207
Book order form 210

Introduction

This is a book written for women, about women and by women. Having said that let me hasten to add that men can enjoy it — and benefit from it — as well. But this book is specifically about what a woman can do to feel confident, be independent and pleased with her life. It assumes you have something in your life that's not working, that in some aspect you're dissatisfied, unhappy and unfulfilled. Perhaps you're at a crossroad or transition in your life. Perhaps you feel you aren't in control of your own destiny. Perhaps you want to change your living environment, career, or your habits or your friends. If there wasn't something that needed changing, you probably wouldn't have invested your money in a method that will help you fix it.

One of the reasons this book may appeal more to women than to men is because of how women approach problem solving. What do men do when a woman communicates a problem? They immediately offer a solution they feel would work and then turn on the ball game. It's not that they're unfeeling. That's just how most men handle any disturbance in their well-ordered lives. Problem? Solution. Next!

Women, on the other hand, don't do as well with quick fixes. We need to see the whole picture, to look at it both logically and emotionally, so we can work out various solutions, trying them one-by-one until we find something really effective. Women have the ability to plan in detail, multi-task and follow-through to the end. At least that's what we do when everything goes as planned.

More often we just throw in the towel and adapt to the situation, no matter how uncomfortable it is. Women who efficiently run a household, raise children, and hold down a job feel they have don't have the resources to turn their situation around. The average woman I talk with operates as a wife, a parent, a teacher, a cook, a nurse, a personal shopper, a budgeting genius, a laundress, a chauffeur, an employee and an amateur psychologist. But when I suggest that she could easily earn the extra income and time that would allow her to enjoy her life, she feels powerless to make even the smallest change.

Why do we feel this way? Based on my experience I think it's because as women we routinely exist with our lives in precarious balance, juggling all the balls we keep in the air, afraid that if we turn our attention to anything new we will lose our rhythm and everything will fall apart.

In addition, women are survivors. In 2003, no less authority than *The New York Times* underlined that fact in an article about men coping with the loss of six-figure jobs in the dot-com crash. Men had difficulty making the transition to retail and manual jobs paying minimum wage. Their self-esteem was negatively impacted. They lost their drive and became clinically depressed. Women, on the other hand, did whatever they had to do to survive and keep the family running. Survival and caring for the family are instincts wired into the female DNA and we're more concerned about survival than status.

Diane and Jim illustrate this. They have a great marriage with what Diane describes as a workable division of labor. "Jim handles the important issues — the U.S. foreign policy, global warming, and the New York Giants' draft picks. I do the little stuff — shopping, laundry, the kids' school activities, cooking…." They remind me of one of my favorite cartoons, two cavemen are discussing a cave woman working in the field. "I hunt, she gathers," one says to the other, "Otherwise we couldn't make ends meet."

Humans, however, have traditionally operated differently. Men have been the hunters, bringing in the food and battling off the predators…until now. During World War II women started stepping into traditional male roles out of necessity. We found we're perfectly capable of holding down a job, putting food on the table, taking care of the family, and, if necessary, living without a man. It's no longer shocking to hear of single women giving birth or adopting a child so they can be a parent outside of typical family infrastructures.

In post-USSR Russia women are leaving their husbands because they don't need them. Japanese women are choosing not to get married at all. In the United States, more and more women put off marriage until their thirties, with many opting to build a career before taking on a family. It's a brand new world for women, our roles have evolved and we have more choices then ever before.

THE *Gimme Five!* METHOD
Q. How do you eat a hippopotamus?
A. One bite at a time!

I designed the *Gimme Five!* Method to help women take control of their lives. Its roots are in that rule we all learned in nursery school, just in case we were ever invited to a hippopotamus feast. What it taught us was that even the biggest project could be dealt with if we break it down into its smallest parts and then handle one part at a time. *Gimme Five!* shows you how to turn your life around, starting with easy "bites" — decisions and exercises that only take *five minutes* to complete. Every one of us can find five minutes, right?

As we go along, the bites get a little larger, the planning takes a little longer, and we look at goals that will take weeks, months or years to achieve. But you can move along at your own pace. There's no rush. No one is holding a clock in front of you.

WHY *Gimme Five!* – Why Now?

I'm often asked why I named my method *Gimme Five!* There are two reasons. First, it reminds me of the universal gesture indicating, "Great job, well done!" — an open-handed slap on another's hand — "*Gimme Five!*" Doing a great job and winning is what this method is all about.

And second, it reminds us to tackle that problem "hippopotamus" one little piece at a time. Five of anything doesn't seem so daunting. We have five fingers on each hand and five toes on each foot. We have five senses. There are five days in the workweek — five major continents — five great lakes. Five is a comfortable number, easily visualized. Five is also a significant number when counting the milestones in our lives. We start school when we're five. We celebrate major achievements — birthdays and anniversaries — in units of five: 30th, 50th, 75th birthday, 25th high school reunion, and 10th, 25th or 50th anniversary. We used to retire at 65 (soon it will be 70 or older). The fifth house in astrology represents the home where a woman keeps everything together. What's more, five in numerology represents FREEDOM — and that's what we're all looking for.

In the Method, we allow you to quickly review your life and your current situation. Too often we're so busy trying to keep our head above water that we don't know what water we're in or how deep it really is. Every chapter will have an exercise, with the first five designed to put you and your current situation in the proper perspective. You can't fix what you don't recognize.

As we move on, the exercises prod you to begin planning the future you have only dreamed about. While it's perfectly okay to change your mind about your dreams and goals as you go along, you need a starting place. Change equals growth, and that's a good thing. What we want to avoid is the all too common situation in which we shy away from change because it represents discomfort, and so we remain in our unhappy rut, convincing ourselves we're powerless to do anything else.

Once the initial dreams are in place we move on to the subject of money. These exercises will show you how you think about money, what it means in your life, how you relate to it, and how you can keep it and grow it.

The fourth part of the *Gimme Five!* Method leads you through your relationships with other people. The exercises allow you to identify the people in your life who can help you achieve your goals and show you how to meet new people, sort out current friends so you spend your time with those who boost you up instead of dragging you down, and then we'll determine what your attitude is and how it's affecting what you do.

In the fifth and final section, we look at the options spread out before you. You can pick and choose which ones will help you solidify your dreams into the reality you wish for. Again, every chapter is followed by an exercise to help you move forward.

In the spirit of five, most exercises and suggestions are short-term activities you can think about without pressure. For instance, if you're trying to replace a bad habit with a healthy one, remember that you can do almost anything for 30 days- it's certainly a more manageable time than a year — or forever. The good news is when you've made a change for 30 days that change is usually permanent. And you don't have to start looking at the full month. Break it down. Stop the habit for five minutes or five hours or five days. Give yourself small intermediate goals that you can attain. Before long, the time has passed and the behavior is modified.

As you move through the book, you'll soon have real progress to celebrate, progress that will surprise and delight you because the results are so immediate. You may be surprised that Chapter 24 shows you how to start planning your exit strategy, when and how you'll step back and smell the roses — or move to other projects that interest you. Every dream should have a deadline at each end. That means a time to start, a time to succeed, and a time to enjoy the success. What too many people don't understand is that you have to start with the end in mind.

The final chapter will serve as a review of what you've learned and done. The exercise asks you to come back in five years and describe where you are and how far you've come. That's right, the last exercise can't be done until the *Gimme Five!* Method has worked for you. (If five years seems like a long time, consider Japan's Sony Corporation. They plan their business five hundred years at a time!) You'll be looking at how your life is when you will have achieved your first goals and how you take your wisdom and knowledge to help someone else define and achieve success.

Throughout, in addition to the exercises and lessons, I'll give you resources you can tap into for further information. You don't have to read all the books and magazines or watch all the films I suggest, but you'll find the more you read, the faster you'll absorb the ideas that will turn your life around for the better. You'll also find website addresses that will give you enormous amounts of information at the click of a mouse — and the songs and movies that crop up in some resource lists give you a way to change your behavior over a bowl of popcorn in your easy chair.

BEEN THERE . . . DONE THAT

First of all, let me assure you that I've done everything I'm suggesting you do. That's how I know it works. I've trained thousands of people — men and women, blue collar and professional workers, U.S. citizens as well as people from Canada, Europe and Asia — so I know the method can be successfully taught to others. I've also learned that as much as we are different, we are alike. We all want love, respect, freedom and peace of mind. Those who followed the *Gimme Five!* Method found it positively altered their lives. Those who stuck with it have achieved incredible things. You'll meet some of them in this book.

As for me, I'm a wife, a mother, and an independent career woman. My parents were strong believers in education. They believed happiness was achieved through a college education, working hard for a large corporation for several decades, and then retiring. You've read the Thought Provoker on page xi. You know that retirement security is a myth.

I worked for major corporations long enough to know a lifetime of meetings and office politics wasn't the existence I wanted. I've had bad relationships. I've been how-do-I-pay-the-rent poor. I've hung with the wrong crowd; I've listened to the wrong people; and I've made unwise decisions. Does this sound familiar?

I'm a first generation American, growing up with immigrant Filipino parents who came to this country after WWII to find a better life for themselves and their children. They instilled strong work ethics and family values in their children. Their mantra was, "Life is what you make it, make the best of it." Today I'm happily married and the mother of two grade-school children, so I have my hands full. They are the greatest joys in my life, and nothing that I could accomplish professionally could ever be as rewarding. My husband is my partner and strongest supporter, but I never expected him to be "my provider."

As a teenager I observed my older cousins marry right out of high school because they had to. (In those days, people got married if they were pregnant.) I watched them struggle through these relationships as debt piled up and work demands and family obligations took their tolls. Often the men stayed out late, drank, gambled and womanized, leaving their wives feeling helpless. These young mothers didn't have the skills or confidence to take care of themselves or their families. I made a decision early on that I wouldn't end up in that situation. Before I was married, I owned my own home and enjoyed a prospering career. I'm perfectly capable of standing on my own two feet … and I want you to have that same peace of mind and sense of accomplishment.

ABOUT THE BOOK

You can probably read this book in a few days, but if you use it correctly it will be your handbook for a lifetime. I want you to keep it like a personal journal. Continue referring to it so your goals are constantly in front of you. It should be the book in your bedside table drawer, always handy for reflection and review, or in your purse or briefcase where you can read and work though the exercises as you're waiting to pick up the kids, in a doctor or dentist's reception room, or on your treadmill exercising. As you work through it, you'll find the *Gimme Five!* Method is quite revealing. It will tell you a lot about who you are, what you believe and where you want to go. The stories will open up your mind to what is possible and encourage you to move forward.

W. Clement Stone, the founder of CNA Insurance and the author of *Success Through a Positive Mental Attitude* and *The Success System that Never Fails,* said that success is achieved by "repetition, repetition, repetition." When you repeat the steps I've taken — those outlined in this book — you'll move along your success path at your own speed. Whatever your personal dream, you have the power to turn it into a reality. You'll see that the key isn't how much education you have or where you live or whom you know. For instance, W. Clement Stone was the son of a widowed mother who he helped support by selling newspapers. No one made it easy for him, but he knew all you need is the desire to make a difference in your circumstances — and the courage to stick to your plan!

This is a personal success book which means it's about you. Not everyone wants to be a millionaire — although if you stick to the *Gimme Five!* Method, it's definitely a possibility. Perhaps your goal is just a few hundred — or a few thousand — extra dollars each month. You may want to stay home and take care of your children without leaving them in the care of sitters. You may want to be totally independent without relying on anyone else's earning power. You may want to buy new clothes or a new car or a new washing machine. You may want to build up a personal nest egg so you can surprise your husband when he thinks about retiring. All that matters is that *you believe* you have the power to achieve your dream. I want you to live the life *you* envision.

Is it always going to be smooth sailing? No. Nothing worthwhile is. But it's not all that difficult if you remember the *Gimme Five!* rules. Like dieting or exercise, it gets easier with every pound lost and every early morning jog. And the final result is certainly ample reward for the time and effort invested.

Section I:
Become Self-Smart

GIMME FIVE! RULE NUMBER ONE

"Know who you are."

❧ CHAPTER ONE ❧

Your Past Doesn't Equal Your Future

> *"If one is lucky, a solitary fantasy can totally transform one million realities."*
> *—Maya Angelou*

IDENTIFY YOUR "POWER WANTS"

There's a Walt Disney song that includes the lyric, "A dream is a wish your heart makes..." The truth is a wish usually is a noise your mouth makes and nothing more.

How many times a day do you start a sentence with "I wish...."? Most of us are always wishing for something ... that it would stop raining, that the basement didn't leak, that we could achieve world peace. Short of moving to the desert, buying a house on a hill, and changing the planet we live on, most of these wishes aren't going to come true anytime soon. And that's the problem.

We're so accustomed to saying "I wish..." — knowing that nothing will happen — that we forget there are a lot of things we can wish for that could come true, even without a fairy godmother. Wish you were a redhead? Dye your hair. Wish you could play the piano? Take lessons. Wish you could wear a smaller size? Close the fridge and take a walk. But just like the major unattainables, these little life wishes aren't taken seriously so nothing ever happens.

The secret to making your dreams or wishes or goals come true is to identify what you really long for, what you have a deep desire for, your

"Power-Wants." A Power-Want is a wish you are willing to work hard to achieve, something that moves you emotionally and passionately, it is something deep in your gut, not a passing whim you think about and forget.

Your Power-Wants are those wishes important enough to you that you would do almost *anything* to make them happen — if you knew what to do. You may have just one Power-Want — or you may have a long list of them. Part of the work in this chapter will be to figure out what you desire badly enough to move past "wistful wish" to Power-Want.

TAKING YOUR LIFE PULSE

Have you learned how to set goals? Has anyone led you through a visualization exercise? Do you know about affirmations and their incredible ability to make your subconscious do the impossible? No one was born with an instruction manual, and most of us have wandered through life picking up lessons from those around us. What do they know? How successful are they?

Don't worry. Whatever you don't know, you'll learn in the next few pages. If you have learned all these techniques, you may unlearn a few of them when you switch to the *Gimme Five!* Method.

However, before you can look at your future, you have to examine your past. Let's not go back too far. I find what's happened over the past five years gives a pretty accurate look at a whole lifetime. We fall into habits and they guide our destinies with pretty fair consistency.

First, I want you to complete the Five-Minute Exercise on page 6. These are simple questions that require simple answers. Don't spend longer than a few minutes working on it. You may want to come back later and add to your answers. That's fine. For now, we just want to examine some immediate impressions and bring them out into the open where you can look at them objectively.

This isn't the time to worry about what you want in the future or what you need to change. This is just an identity check. It will tell you what your life is like on a day-to-day basis. Next to each question I've given you some trigger words to stimulate your thinking. Your answers may be totally different than mine or any other woman's, and that's just fine. You are a unique person and only you can identify your triggers.

Remember, these questions should be answered with respect to only the past five years of your life. Never mind about grade school or what happened in 1994.

My friend Patricia Wiklund, Ph.D., is a psychologist who had a down-to-earth approach to problems long before Dr. Phil came along. On the couch in her living room is an embroidered pillow that sums up her approach to a bad past. It says, "GET OVER IT!" Pat knows what she's talking about. She's been through a lot of ugliness in her life. Her mother died of breast cancer when she was ten. Her first book told about her psychologist husband whose phone call from jail was her first inkling he was a pedophile. She raised her son as a single parent. She gave up her career to nurse her father through his final 18 months and then had to re-establish herself. And still she says with a big smile, "Get over it!" In other words, stop ruining your life, reducing your potential because of things you couldn't control in your past.

Forgive yourself and others, realize you can't change others or your past; it's the only way to move on. Free yourself from the bondage of hate, anger, resentment, guilt and shame. Once you make the decision — "If it is to be, it's up to me" — you'll find yourself soaring forward. Just as the pilot in a jet doesn't have a rearview mirror, if you don't look back you can fly to the heights of success and happiness. Sure it takes courage, but you can do it. Move on!

You have zero control over the past, but you do have control over your future. You can make a decision to move on as quickly as you choose. Decide it's time for a new story, a better story. Is it possible to change? Have others in your position been able to change? Yes! It's just easier not to. I know so many people who have chosen to change and made their lives and the lives of others so much happier.

Sarah was molested by her grandfather when she was six. Ashamed to tell anyone, she lived in pain and guilt while she battled with self-confidence, weight and relationship issues throughout her adult years and into her married life. Sarah is beautiful, witty and successful. No one would have ever guessed the dark secret that was destroying her marriage. She trusted no one and certainly didn't want to have children who could also be abused. After attending a workshop and discovering how many people were suffering residual insecurities and fears, she was able to forgive her grandfather, free herself from her past, and move on. Today she is happily married and the mother of three children.

You may have had an alcoholic mother, an abusive boyfriend, a drug-addicted sister, a tyrannical boss ... whoever has made the past uglier than it could have been, forgive and move on. If you've had challenges with anger, shame, resentment, feelings of regret or inadequacy ... now is the time to put them behind you. Sarah is just one of hundreds and hundreds of people who have made the decision to change, to forgive herself and others, and to summon the courage to move on. She's a living example that your past doesn't have to equal your future. Just examine your recent history. Nothing else really matters. We can't change our past, but we can sure determine our future!

FIVE-MINUTE EXERCISE #1

Where do you live? *(House? Apartment? City? Rural area?)* _____

_____

What is your family like? *(Alone? Married? Children? Ages?)*_____

_____

What type of work do you do? *(Career? Self-employed? Homemaker?)*_____

_____

Who do you hang out with? *(Friends? Family? Co-workers? Loner?)* _____

_____

What have you accomplished? *(Children? Work? Community? Church?)* _____

_____

_____

What is your health situation? *(Medical problems? Overweight? Stressed?)* ___

_____

_____

What is your financial situation? *(Struggling? Comfortable? Bleak?)* _____

_____

_____

_____

What part does spirituality or religion play in your life? _____

_____

What is your lifestyle? _(Single? Working wife/mother? Single mother? Student?)_

_____

What is your happiness quotient? _(On scale of 1–10 where 1 is miserable and 10 is terrific.)_ _____

What part does spirituality or religion play in your life? _____

_____

What is your lifestyle? _(Single? Working wife/mother? Single mother? Student?)_

_____

What is your happiness quotient? _(On scale of 1–10 where 1 is miserable and 10 is terrific.)_ _____

ANY ANSWER IS CORRECT

There are no right or wrong answers to any exercise in this book. What's right for me might be wrong for you and vice-versa. The important thing is that you are always honest with yourself. If you lie to you, there's no one you can ever trust.

I would make one observation on the last question about your happiness quotient. If you answered that you're a 10, then why are you reading this book? That's right. People who are perfectly content with their lives aren't the top audience for self-development books and seminars. If you're totally happy, keep doing what you're doing and give this book to someone who needs it. I'll bet there are a lot of potential recipients right on your block.

ARE WE NUTS?

DEFINITION OF INSANITY:
Doing the same thing over and over again and expecting a different result.

Think about it. If you put your hand on a hot stove and get burned, you'd have to be crazy to think you could do it again and not be burned the second time. In the physical world we learn very quickly what we should avoid. The wise child only needs to break her leg once jumping off the roof before learning to stay on the ground. In the rest of our lives, we aren't so smart.

> _If the extra helping of pasta put weight on me yesterday, maybe it won't today._

> _If I'm tired because I stayed up watching cable movies until two this morning, maybe I can do it again tonight and feel fine._

> _If my boyfriend slapped me once, maybe he'll never do it again._

We build our lives on the shaky foundation of "Maybe Mistakes." Unfortunately, for every "maybe," there's a "But Probably" lurking in the shadows.

> _If I skip my exercises today, maybe I'll do them tomorrow...but probably I'll be too busy._

> _If I drop out of night school this semester, maybe I'll go back next fall....but probably I'll have another job by then._

Candy is a good example of someone who bet on the "maybe" and lost on the "probably."

Candy is a very attractive woman and a brilliant attorney. All she wants is a loving relationship and a fulfilling marriage. When her husband announced he wanted a divorce, her world was shattered. He wouldn't go to counseling. He didn't want to make it work. He wanted out now.

"Maybe he'll come back," she thought, but after months hoping to reconcile and fighting bouts with depression while watching her ex-husband date other women, Candy realized probably it was over.

Then she met Larry, loving and attentive with a great sense of humor. As aggressive as she could be in a courtroom, Candy was very shy in relationships. She wanted children. Larry was very easy to be with. Maybe this would work.

More than a year into the relationship, Larry had been laid off and was working odd jobs. How was Candy? She wasn't fulfilled, but the relationship didn't take a lot of work and maybe it was better than having to go back to dating. If she left him, probably she would have to start all over again and she just didn't have the energy.

Almost 15 years later, Candy is still with Larry, who lives in her house and works on-and-off when he feels like it. Maybe they'll never get married and probably 49-year-old Candy will never have the children she wished for.

Go back over your first exercise. Which of these things are you hoping maybe will change — but probably won't? Take a colored pen and put a check mark next to the circumstances of your life that you would like to be different. Don't worry now about how you're going to accomplish these changes. We'll get to that a little later on.

SUGGESTED RESOURCES

Books:

Taking Charge When You Are Not in Control by Patricia Wiklund, Ph.D. (Ballantine, 2000 — ISBN: B00005BBWB) Available as an Adobe format download or from used book dealers on Amazon.com.

Self-Matters, Creating Your Life from the Inside Out by Dr. Philip McGraw (Simon & Schuster; 2001 — ISBN: 074322423X)

Forgive for Good: A Proven Prescription for Health and Happiness by Dr. Fred Luskin (HarperSanFrancisco; 2001 - ISBN: 0062517201) and director of the Stanford University Forgiveness Project www.learningtoforgive.com

Film:

Divine Secrets of the Ya-Ya Sisterhood with Sandra Bullock, Ellen Burstyn

Song:

Forgiveness by Don Henley

Cable TV:

The Biography Channel features famous people, past and present and stories of their triumph over adversities, fears and failures. www.biography.com provides products and programming schedule for the Biography channel.

ᏃᏒ CHAPTER TWO ᏔᏂᏇ

What Do You Consider Success? Happiness?

> *You have to count on living every single day in a way you believe will make you feel good about your life — so that if it were over tomorrow, you'd be content with yourself.*
> *—Jane Seymour*

EVERYONE DEFINES IT DIFFERENTLY

There is no one definition of success or happiness. Basically, it could be said your success is what you've accomplished. Your happiness is how you feel about your life. But even these definitions are up for discussion.

Each of us has to define success and happiness for ourselves. What makes you feel as if you've conquered the mountain may leave me feeling unfulfilled. What lights up your world may be of no interest to your best friend. Each of us is an individual and our perceptions of the world are just as individual as we are.

Many years ago, an elementary school teacher conducted a study that has become classic in education. She divided her classroom into two groups. One group, the brown-eyed children were told they were smarter than their blue-eyed classmates. They were assured they had better minds, higher IQs, and were expected to do better on tests. The blue-eyed kids were told they couldn't hope to achieve on the same level as the brown-eyed boys and girls.

Over the course of a week, the grades of the two groups were registered. The brown-eyed children, including some who had learning challenges, excelled at everything they did. Test scores were up. Their hands were always in the air. They were shouting out correct answers. The blue-eyed children were hardly noticeable. Their scores plummeted. They didn't even try.

At the end of the week, the teacher apologized. "I made a mistake," she said. "I misread the report. Actually, it's you blue-eyed children who are smarter and higher achievers." As you might guess, over the following week the scores of the two groups reversed. The blue-eyes now controlled the curve and led in the learning activities.

Finally, the teacher explained what she had done and taught her class that they must never allow anyone else's opinion affect their self-esteem or hamper their striving to succeed. It doesn't matter how important someone appears to be or how scientific their reports might seem. The only person who controls what you are capable of doing is you.

In the same vein, motivational speaker Les Brown tells how he was put in a class for special learners because he was "stupid." He believed it, until the woman who became his adoptive mother mainstreamed him and convinced him he was smarter than anyone else around. I doubt any of the so-called experts in Cleveland's school system who rated the young orphan below par academically has made a tenth of the money Les Brown has. So much for "expert" opinions! Who you are and who you will be is up to you.

Julie considers herself a success because she never graduated from high school but earned a Ph.D. Although she's never made more than $30,000 a year teaching, her joy is in having overcome her early mistake of leaving school to get married and start a family. By earning her degrees, she proved she was as smart as anyone. Money isn't her success barometer.

* * * * * * * * *

Deborah is crippled with multiple sclerosis but she's the most cheerful person you'll ever meet. She says she's happy the disease didn't hit until she was in her fifties so she had half a decade to run around before she was confined to a wheelchair. When she wins the bingo game at her assisted living center, you can hear her joyful laugh from across the room.

* * * * * * * * *

Susan is an Olympic athlete and her definition of success is crossing the finish line, no matter how long it takes her. She competes in the Special Olympics.

* * * * * * * * *

Mary calls her friends to share her happiness when the Chicago Cubs win a ball game. That's all it takes to make her smile from ear to ear.

You get the idea. No two people feel the same. Your reality is the world as YOU see it, not the way it's reported in the papers or represented on the nightly news.

Success can be a huge achievement or simply mastering email. Happiness doesn't mean everything's rosy and there aren't any problems. As one wise person said, "Happiness is not an absence of conflict, but the ability to cope with it." It all boils down to how you feel about yourself and what you've done in your life. In both cases, attitude has a lot to do with it and attitude is something we'll talk about a lot later on.

For right now, go to the exercise on the next page. Take five minutes and write down what makes you feel successful and what makes you feel happy. They probably won't be the same things. I know a woman who was grinning from ear to ear the day she successfully learned to parallel park her SUV. "I'm so happy," she crowed.

The real successes in life — and the things that make us the happiest — often seem inconsequential to everyone else. Remember, each of us is a different and unique individual. That's what is really important!

Suggested Resources:

Books:

Finding Your Own North Star: Claiming the Life You Were Meant to Live, by Martha Beck (Three Rivers Press, New York, NY 2001 ISBN: 0-8129-3218-8)

Authentic Happiness: Using the New Positive Psychology to Realize Your Potential for Lasting Fulfillment, by Martin Seligman. (Free Press: 2002 — ISBN: 0743222970)

The Law of Success In Sixteen Lessons, by Napoleon Hill (Wilshire Book Co., 2000 — ISBN: 0879804475)

Live Your Dreams by Les Brown, (William Morrow & Co, 1992 — ISBN:0688118895)

FIVE-MINUTE EXERCISE #2

I feel I'm a success when _____

_____

_____

_____

_____

_____

I feel happy when _____

_____

_____

_____

_____

_____

_____

_____

𝕰𝕸 CHAPTER THREE 𝕳𝕹

How to Set a Course and Follow It

> *I am not afraid of storms for I am learning*
> *how to sail my ship.*
> *–Louisa May Alcott*

HOW DID YOU GET WHERE YOU ARE TODAY?

It's been said, "Life is what happens when you're making other plans." The fact is most of us didn't make the other plans, we just climbed aboard the ship and let life take us where it wanted. The idea of laying out a course and steering in a specific direction never occurred to us — or if it did it seemed like too much effort.

The problem is if you don't know where you're going, I promise you'll get there….nowhere. I was reading Alice in Wonderland to my daughter the other day and I came across this bit of conversation.

Alice:	*Would you tell me, please, which way I ought to walk from here?*
Cheshire Cat:	*That depends a good deal on where you want to get to.*
Alice:	*I don't care much where -*
Cheshire Cat:	*Then it doesn't matter which way you walk.*

The grinning cat had no doubts about it. If you don't know where you're going, it doesn't much matter which direction you take to get there.

WHICH KIND OF PERSON ARE YOU?

How much of your life have you planned out? Before you start planning the future, I want you to look more closely at the past. Where have you been? What have you done? How much of it was planned in advance and how much just happened?

There are three kinds of people. First, we have those who are in the game, actively participating and making things happen. Then we have the life spectators who applaud others, marvel at their accomplishments and criticize their performance as they watch the game comfortably in their seats. Finally, there is the third group — and to me, they are the saddest. They don't even know the game is being played. They're just outside the stadium cruising through life on autopilot, taking whatever is handed to them, continually complaining and ultimately blaming everyone else for their meager existence.

In the Bible it says, "Seek and you shall find." My version of that is, "You don't get what you don't ask for."

We're always asking for equality with men. Well, we got it and we're stuck with it. In the 21st century, don't count on Prince Charming riding up to the front door on his white horse, scooping you up and taking you to live at the castle. It's the stuff of movies like *Pretty Woman*. Today, we're responsible for ourselves. No one is going to do it for us. That's the good news. Today we can do anything we want without asking a man for permission. But notice that verb, "do." If you don't *do* something, nothing is going to get any better.

Everyone is at a different stage when they pick up this book. There are chapters that will turn on light bulbs and allow you to see things as you never saw them before. There are things you've heard before but, for some reason, today the message finally resonates through you. If you read this book but skip the exercises, pay no attention to the resources, and are not open to learning, preferring to constantly criticize the method, I guarantee you won't make much progress.

Annette used to work at a company that produced self-improvement audiotapes. When a disgruntled customer called and complained that he had bought over $1000 worth of tapes and his life hadn't changed, she explained his problem. "Outside my window," she said, "it's sleeting and the streets are ice-covered. We're looking at another six or eight weeks of winter. In this building, every employee listens to our tapes. Some of us are in positions where we've listened to them multiple times. Believe me, if it were possible to benefit from the advice without getting out of my chair, I'd be in Cancun right now instead of in Chicago. If you don't make the changes in your behavior that the tapes suggest, nothing's going to be any different, no matter how much money you spend."

Annette told me it used to disturb her when people spent so much money buying books and tapes and attending seminars but weren't willing to make the necessary personal changes. "They're like self-help junkies," she said. "They want "the fix" but they don't want to work to fix the problem they're buying the fix for."

This is a decision each of us has to make. Because of the work I do, I attend a number of seminars, read a lot of books, and listen to countless audios, all designed to make me a better person. The only ones that have made a noticeable impact are those that presented suggestions I took the time and effort to adapt for my life.

If you bought this book, you've probably bought others. The last thing you want to become is one of Annette's "self-help junkies" who can't get enough because you're too busy hearing and reading and seeing to go out and do anything! That's self-defeating.

For your next Five-Minute Exercise, I want you to look at the events in your life that brought you to where you are now. You'll see it looks somewhat like a résumé and that's deliberate. It's helpful to look at our lives spread out on one sheet of paper. Suddenly we see choices and patterns and obstacles we never saw before.

Take your time but don't agonize over your answers. One of the wonders of life is that nothing but our headstone is carved in granite. Everything else can be altered, changed and rearranged.

You'll find there are some hints as to the kind of information you need to put down in the exercise, but as always, your answers may be totally different than anyone else's. Be honest with yourself and you may get a surprise.

Suggested Resources:

Books:

Simple Abundance, by Sarah Ban Breathnach (Warner Books, 1995 — ISBN: 0446519138)

Lifemaps: A Step-By-Step Method for Simplifying 101 of Life's Most Overwhelming Projects by Michael Antoniak, Stephen M. Pollan (Editor), Mark Levine (Editor)(Fireside; 2002 — ISBN: 0743400615)

FIVE-MINUTE EXERCISE #3A

What is your education level? *(High school? Junior college? University? Graduate school?)* _____

Relationship situation? *(Married, divorced, parent, widowed, single)* _____
_____

Living situation? *(With family? Alone? Parents? Roommates?)* _____
_____

Has anything major changed in the past five years in your relationship or living situation? _____
_____

Why did you choose your current work? *(Further your career? Need to cover bills? Wanted career change?)* _____
_____

What chain of events led you to where you are now? *(Career / job? Marriage? Parenthood? Friends?)* _____
_____

If I could have done something differently, I would have _____
_____
_____

FIVE-MINUTE EXERCISE #3B: MY LIFE TIMELINE

Where were you living, what were you doing, who were you with at these five year milestones in your life. Do you see any patterns in your life?

Age 5_____

_____

Age 10_____

_____

Age 15_____

_____

Age 20_____

_____

Age 25_____

_____

Age 30_____

_____

Age 35_____

_____

Age 40_____

_____

Age 45_____

_____

Age 50_____

_____

Age 55_____

_____

Age 60_____

_____

Age 65_____

_____

THOUGHT PROVOKER: TOMORROW IS TOO LATE

The truth is there's no better time than now to change your life and be happy. If not now, when? Your life will always be filled with challenges.

It's best to admit this, decide to treasure every moment you have, and remember there will never be a better time to begin to realize your dreams than today ...because time waits for no one.

So, stop waiting ...

- Until your car or home is paid off.
- Until you get a new car or home.
- Until your kids leave the house.
- Until you go back to school.
- Until you finish school.
- Until you lose 10 lbs.
- Until you gain 10 lbs.
- Until you get married.
- Until you get a divorce.
- Until you have kids.
- Until you retire.
- Until Winter.
- Until Spring.
- Until Summer.
- Until Fall.
- Until you die.

There is no better time than right now to be happy and realize your dreams. Happiness is a journey, not a destination.

Work like you don't need money,
Love like you've never been hurt, and
Dance like no one's watching.
(adapted from anonymous Internet posting)

❧ CHAPTER FOUR ❧

Building Your Belief and Taking a Leap Of Faith

When I look into the future, it's so bright it burns my eyes.
—Oprah Winfrey

THE OPRAH PHENOMENON

Since I have quoted Oprah, I think we should take a minute and remember that no one handed her fame and fortune on a silver platter. Today, she is one of the wealthiest women in America but she began life far differently. She was born out-of-wedlock and lived with a succession of relatives before her father took her in. She was raped by her cousin, and then sexually molested both by an uncle and by a family friend. She was too ashamed to tell anyone or to try and protect herself. Like most abused children, she thought it was her fault.

She came from a poor family and had to work hard for everything she ever got. She tells this story about when she was just four years old. "I remember standing on the back porch — it was a screened-in porch — and my grandmother was boiling clothes ... in a great big iron pot...and poking them down. I was watching her ... and I remember thinking, my life won't be like this. My life won't be like this, it will be better."

She admits she didn't know then what the future would hold, but she had begun to develop her vision. She knew what she *didn't* want and what she *had to* change. That's the crucial first step.

One of the complaints I hear most often is, "I know what I want but I don't know how to get it." It's a common problem with a three-step solution.

STEP 1: GAIN CLARITY THROUGH KNOWING WHAT YOU DON'T WANT

I've found people often have difficulty writing down what they want but they can sure go on and on about what they don't want:

- *I don't want to work for anyone else,*
- *I don't want to commute an hour to work,*
- *I don't want my kids to go to this school,*
- *I don't want friends who just whine, complain and drain my energy.*
- *I don't want an empty relationship.*

If you have trouble figuring out what you want, write down all the things you don't want. Then turn each of those don'ts into what you do want:

- *I want to be self-employed,*
- *I want to work from my home,*
- *I want to afford moving to a different school district or pay for private schools,*
- *I want to surround myself with positive, forward thinking, motivating friends.*
- *I want a loving, supportive and nurturing relationship.*

Writing down what you want is the first step in realizing your goals. The experts call it visualization but to the rest of us, it's dreaming… the written words lead us to picturing what we want in our minds so clearly that we can reach out and touch it, smell it and taste it.

Pretend you're an artist and could paint the picture of your ideal existence. You need to be very specific in every detail. Leave nothing to chance. That means, instead of saying you'd like a new car, say you'd like a bright red Porsche convertible with black leather seats, a CD player, and white walls. The more detail you can include, the more real it will become. That's step one.

If you can't imagine what you want, look through magazines and cut out pictures of your Power-Wants — the rooms you'd like to live in, the car you want to drive, the clothes you want to wear, the neighborhood where you want to live, the vacation spots you'd like to visit.

Darlene and her husband bought a lot by a lake where they had planned to build their dream home. Dan was a pilot with a good but modest income and Darlene was at home with their four small children. At the time they didn't know how they would be able to afford to build their dream home, they just focused on the home of their dreams with everything they would want in it and moved forward with architectural plans, space design, room colors — envisioning and putting on paper everything down to wall fixtures and electrical outlets. Darlene's desire to work out of her home and earn money took a few years of trying different home businesses and eventually paid off big time when she starting marketing telecommunication services and training independent reps to do the same. It took fifteen years and today they live in their dream home. What a thrill it was to send out their Christmas cards with the whole family in front of their now very real dream home.

STEP 2: MAKE YOUR FUTURE BOOK

I suggest you make a Future Book. To do this, take a notebook or binder and have your written statements of what you want in it and paste in the pictures you've collected of your Power Wants. On the cover, announce it as your own: _____'s Future. (My book says "Josie's Future" and I'm still adding to it.) When you can see your dreams in front of you as you turn the pages of your book, they will begin to be very real.

When you're planning your future, don't give a thought to your current situation. If you rent an apartment in New Jersey and drive a ten-year-old car but you want to own a condo on the beach in Florida and drive a Mustang convertible, go for it. Don't let worries about how you'll get there or how you'll afford your new life get in the way of planning for your new life.

Napoleon Hill wrote the classic book *Think and Grow Rich* while working for the steel magnate, Andrew Carnegie. After interviewing 500 millionaires, he came up with the common denominator for success. He said that we can achieve whatever we're able to "conceive and believe." That means applying the "I x V^2 = R Principle." *Imagination* multiplied by *Vivid Vision* equals *Reality*. When what you dream of seems completely touchable and attainable, it will become real.

* * * * * * * * *

Jane was excited about starting her new business and while she was getting it started, she met Mike. I'll never forget Jane and Mike's Future

Book. She put it together with pictures of their dream houses and dream lifestyle. Five years later, the relationship had ended, but Jane never lost sight of her dream.

Over dinner one evening she told me about a guy she was dating who invited her to go on a leisurely walk in the hills around San Francisco Bay. Suddenly she stopped dead in her tracks and stared at the massive compound spread out below them. When her date asked what she was looking at, she said, "That's the house, my dream house. I cut that picture out of *Architectural Digest* five years ago. He claimed he knew the owners and could take her to see it. It turned out he owned the house. Furthermore, he had written out five pages describing his dream life mate. She matched every word perfectly. Jane is now a fervent believer in the magic of Power Wants kept alive in a personal Future Book.

STEP 3: BUILD YOUR BELIEF

Have you ever heard someone say; "I always get good parking spaces" or "I always win the door prize"? These are people who have a high level of expectancy, a spiritual component and one key to building your belief and getting what you want. It can be difficult to be positive when you feel low and your current conditions reflect nothing of the life you desire. Building your belief is building your confidence, the opposite of fear and doubt. Whatever you believe today has been a process of hearing something, experiencing something and telling yourself something over and over again. Perhaps you invested in a stock that you received a "hot tip" on and lost all that you invested. You have never made money in the market, you've never felt comfortable with the stock market and with this experience you know you'll never be good at investing. That's what you tell yourself over and over and that's what you believe. The good news is you can change your thoughts, and you can change your beliefs and create a new reality for yourself.

A practical component to building your belief is to look for evidence of success and ask yourself, "Has anyone ever done this? How did they do it? What did they know?" Next, commit to building your knowledge, accessing the resources, contacting the experts and performing the activities to help build your confidence. Do people make money in the market? Absolutely. Every day people make hundreds of dollars in the market. There are thousands of people that make hundreds of thousands of dollars each and every month. There are classes I can take, computer tools I can access, periodicals to read and use for researching and experts I can consult with.

Judy has always loved the outdoors and nature hikes. After moving to a new area, she discovered a wonderful state park nearby with miles and miles of hiking trails and absolutely beautiful views of the valley below. When she thought about going for a hike, at first she became fearful about getting lost with no one to look for her. She immediately calmed herself down and thought; "People walk these trails every day, probably hundreds of people walk them every week, thousands every month. No one has ever been lost. I can get a map of the park before I start out and walk just 15 minutes up and back the same trail or I can find someone who knows the trails to tell me more about them and perhaps even walk with me. I can walk with my cell phone in the event I may need help."

Judy found she was able to build her belief and confidence by looking for evidence (has anyone done this before me?), getting the knowledge, (contacting someone who has accomplished what you want to do), and preparing herself prior to her walk by carrying her cell phone and going for a short, safe walk first. Taking these simple small steps has led her a newfound confidence and a network of friends who now meet regularly to take six-mile hikes.

* * * * * * * * *

Janice was divorced after 13 years of marriage. With the help of a community development program, she was able to own her own home, and today she owns her second home and a successful business that has supported her family for six years.

"When I bought my first little house in Florida, I had no job, no savings, and didn't even have the money for next month's rent on the house I was living in! Before the loan went through, when I would go to sleep at night I would imagine myself in the house, in the kitchen. I could see the colors — I could *feel* myself there. Soon, the house was mine.

"My first night in my new home, as I fell into exhausted yet euphoric sleep, I realized I was living what I had previously imagined. It was a big breakthrough for me. I began to believe that if I envisioned myself somewhere, that

I could get there. But, if I couldn't envision myself somewhere, that I likewise could NOT get there. What a simple, yet life-changing revelation!"

The faster you take the steps to build your belief, the sooner you will realize your dreams. In your Future Book write down the evidence that supports your belief. Chronicle people, things and events that are helping you move forward.

> _"The future belongs to those who believe_
> _in the beauty of their dreams"._
> _—Eleanor Roosevelt_

For this exercise, time, money, and relationships are no obstacle. You're free and clear of every obligation and hindrance. Where would you go, how would you live, what would you do, who would you do it with?

Don't think about when this is going to happen. For now, you're like an architect designing a building. You can imagine how it's going to look and how the landscaping will add to it, but it's just an idea on paper. While it may take years before the building is finally erected, decorated, furnished, and landscaped, the architect sees it as fully developed.

That's how you have to look at your Power-Want vision for the future — as if it already waiting for you to arrive and move in. Keep your Future Book where you can look at it — and add to it or subtract from it as your tastes and goals change — anytime you feel the urge.

In the next exercise, you should begin the planning for the future process by writing down what you want in some of the basic areas of your life. Be prepared for these to change as you go along. Sometimes what we think we want doesn't look as appealing when it's close to being a reality. Never be afraid to revise your dream.

Suggested Resources:

Books:

The Uncommon Wisdom of Oprah Winfrey: A Portrait in Her Own Words by Oprah Winfrey, Bill Adler (Editor) (Morrow: 1996 — ISBN: 0-688-14382-2)

The Magic of Getting What You Want by David J. Schwartz (Wm. Morrow & Company: 1983 — ISBN: 0-688-01824-6)

Magazines:

O Magazine, Oprah Winfrey, founder and executive editor. Monthly on newsstands or by subscription.

FIVE-MINUTE EXERCISE #4A: Start your Future Book today!

If I didn't have to worry about time or money, I would . . .
Look Like (physically) _____
Have in the bank_____
(be specific about $ amount in savings/checking)
Shop at _____
Live at _____
Live with _____
Drive_____
Work_____
Do for fun_____
Travel/Vacation _____

FIVE-MINUTE EXERCISE #4B

By making a list of what you want to do, be, have, accomplish, you'll find that one by one, events and people in your life will help make these a reality.

If I didn't have to worry about time or money, I would _____
_____
_____

CHAPTER FIVE

The Secret to Getting Focused and Staying Motivated

> *Reach high, for stars lie hidden in your soul. Dream deep, for every dream precedes the goal.*
> *—Pamela Vaull Starr*

FIND YOUR "WHY" AND IT WILL MOTIVATE YOU

What would be worth the sacrifice needed to accomplish one or all of your Power-Wants? For women to invest time and effort in a dream or goal, we first have to understand why it's important to us. We're accustomed to putting ourselves second, taking care of ourselves only after everyone else is satisfied. Before we treat ourselves, we have to know that what we're doing has a legitimate reason.

It's time for women to put ourselves first. I know it's hard. Self-care needs to be a priority in your life. We've all heard a flight attendant instruct us that in the event of an emergency, when oxygen masks drop down, the adults should put on their masks first, and then put them on the children. This goes against our instinct to put our youngsters' well being ahead of our own. The truth is that we have to help ourselves first so we can help others. It's sound advice we need to embrace in other areas of our life.

As a wife, mother, daughter and sister, I am very well acquainted with the emotional and physical demands we face. It's hard to be always available for all the people we love who need us, but as Dr. Phil McGraw reminds his audiences, "If Mama's not happy, nobody's happy."

When we feel that our lives are empty and we're not getting what we want, it's hard to maintain a cheerful, upbeat attitude. Our depression or resentment or exhaustion is transferred to those around us, who in turn pass it on to those around them. It's a vicious cycle. As one friend said, "Yeah, and if everyone else is miserable that's our fault, too." She's right. When it's time to hand out the blame, there's always a woman ready to take it.

Enough! It's time to get our power back. That's what the *Gimme Five!* Method is designed to do. When I tell you what you have to do, it's because I've had to do it. I've tested the Method ... members of my audiences have tested the Method...and we know it works. Let me tell you my story.

In 1995, when I started my current business, I was a stay-at-home mom with a young son and money was very tight. I wanted to have another child and still be able to be home with my family, but I didn't want my husband Joe to work three jobs to provide the quality of life that includes nice clothes, a big house in a good neighborhood, and family vacations taken whenever we wanted.

I knew I would have to work hard to achieve the kind of success that would generate a residual income at a level permitting me to stay home. Residual income is money that comes in regularly, even when you're not working. For instance, book and CD royalties paid to authors and musicians are residual income. The work is done once and it continues to pay off. Well, if it works for them, it should work for me.

This concept is all but foreign to those of us who have been indoctrinated into the 40/40 plan (working 40 years for 40 hours only to retire on what was too little to begin with!) I began to question this plan about five years into my corporate career. I was working a lot of hours and making good money, yet I couldn't see doing this for the next four decades so I could retire at sixty-five. It was even more shocking to look at the people who had been there 20, 30 and 40 years. I didn't like what I saw.

I told my accountant how depressed I was by the vision of a life spent working for other people. He said most of his clients would love to be in my position, earning a "good" salary with a "good" company. I continued to think of how I could possibly get to a position where I could make my own choices without money being a constant issue.

Then I was introduced to two women, both single mothers. One was quietly accumulating real estate and the other was building a distribution business. Both were working out of their homes and were in the top 3% of income earners. They had the freedom to participate in their children's school activities, attend their school functions, and only work when and if they chose. I was eager to have them teach me how to accumulate property and build a business that generated residual income.

Until this time, if I worked I got paid. My salary was entirely dependent on my continual effort. I wanted a lifestyle that allowed me the time to be with my children, provide them with a great education, and enjoy the good life. Sounds impossible, right? Not at all!

I went into business for myself. I kept a picture of my son — and later my daughter — in the front of my Daytimer™ and looked at it whenever I opened my book to set an appointment or attend a meeting. Many times I missed being home when the kids got up and often Joe put them to bed without me. It was a tremendous sacrifice but I always kept the Why in the front of my mind. My children and family were worth every bit of the sacrifice. I was doing it for them.

I kept the vision of the coming days when we could turn off the alarm clock, go to the park and have picnics, or just walk to the bookstore and read together. I knew what I had to do and I had a definite time frame I had to do it in.

I missed my original financial independence goal date because I took six months off for maternity leave when my daughter was born. Then I went back to work to finish the job. Nine months later I was home for good. Like a third child, I'd given birth to a business that brought me residual income month after month, year after year, while I was a full-time wife and mother.

Today, my reputation in the business still stands and I'm often asked to help build new companies and give training sessions for others so they can duplicate my success. I'm happy to do that, but now I pick and choose what I do and when I do it. That's the kind of freedom I want you to have too!

My "Why" was being home with my family. Your Why may be very different. Whether you want independence so you can travel, or buy a new house, or put your kids through college, care for an aging parent or pay for plastic surgery, or retire comfortably with your husband, or purchase a vacation home — whatever it is that moves you, make sure it's big enough and emotional enough and real enough so you don't quit when things get tough.

And they will get tough. I can promise you that. Nothing great happens without effort. The good news is we cherish the things we sacrifice for so much more than we appreciate what falls into our laps.

In the front of your Future Book, either write out or put a picture of the Why that's driving you. It can be a picture of your kids or your family — or it can be a mirror so you remember that you're doing this for you — and that's perfectly fine. You are as valid a Why as any other reason in this world.

And in another section of the book start a Win List. This is a list of everything you do right, every success — no matter how insignificant it seems at the time — and every tiny goal you have reached. This is like "Grandma's Brag Book" only it's about you and what you've done. There's no better motivator than success. There's nothing that will spur you to new successes as surely as your previous pay-offs, so don't be modest. Write down every little triumph — and then revisit the list every day. You don't want to forget a single precious winning moment. Before long, the list will run many pages and your self-esteem and self-confidence will be higher than ever before. You'll know there's nothing that can stop you!

> Comic Jim Carrey proved how effective it is to keep your goal in front of yourself at all times. In the late 1980s, he was finding it difficult to get work. His career was going nowhere. He visualized what it would be like to make a lot of money and have the stardom he hungered after.
>
> Rather than just dream, Carrey wrote himself a check for $10,000,000 — that's right, ten million dollars — and he dated it Thanksgiving Day, 1995. He put the check in his wallet where he'd see it several times a day. When he was discouraged, he would take out the check and look at it, imagining what his life would be like when he could back up that check with cash.
>
> By Thanksgiving, 1995, he had been offered ten million dollars to star in *Mask 2*. A year later, that was doubled for *The Cable Guy*. Would it have happened without the check? Maybe. But his specific goal and concentration on it certainly had a great deal with turning his vision into reality.

Napoleon Hill, the author of *Think and Grow Rich* and other books that have been read and quoted since the 1920s, called this "Definiteness of Purpose." It means you're moving past "woulda, coulda, shoulda" and into "gonna now!"

On the next page, I've left you some space to write down your reasons for changing your life and making yourself financially independent. You can jot down words or write sentences or, if you're not quite sure what your Why is, just let your thoughts spill out randomly. When you come back to it after a day or two, you'll probably see a pattern in what you've written. We usually know the Why, but we don't always know how to express it.

When you've isolated your Why, make certain you keep a symbol of it posted in several places to remind you. It can be a picture or a single word or a symbol that you tack up inside your closet door or keep in your handbag or stick on the visor in your car or put on the refrigerator. You want to see it and remember it often every day. Keeping your focus laser sharp will nudge you forward in the direction of your new life and keep you motivated through tough days.

SUCCESS TECHNIQUE #1:

Keep your "WHY" visible, so that you can see it several times throughout the day.

Suggested Resources:
Books:

Think and Grow Rich, by Napoleon Hill (Fawcett Books; Reissue ed., 1990 — ISBN: 0449214923)

The Millionaire Mind by Thomas J. Stanley, Ph.D. (Andrews McMeel Publishing: 2000 — ISBN: 0-7407-0357-9)

The Magic of Thinking Big by David J. Schwartz, Ph.D. (Simon & Schuster, Inc. 1987 — ISBN: 0-671-64678-8)

FIVE-MINUTE EXERCISE #5: A PICTURE IS WORTH A THOUSAND WORDS AND CAN CARRY YOU THROUGH TOUGH TIMES.

My Why Reason for investing time and effort into making my dream come true is_____

_____

_____

_____

_____

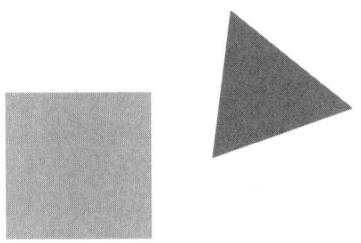

Section II:
Become Vision- and Goal-Smart

GIMME FIVE! RULE NUMBER TWO

**"You are who you think you are
– but you will be who you believe
you will be."**

CHAPTER SIX

See and Say Your Dream into Reality

> *The best time to plant a tree was 20 years ago.*
> *The second best time is now.*
> *– Chinese Proverb*

TODAY IS THE FIRST DAY OF THE REST OF YOUR LIFE

I love that proverb because it reminds me of the bamboo plants in my yard in California. Bamboo growing isn't for the impatient. You often tend to the stalks for over a year before they suddenly begin to shoot up, seemingly growing inches in a day. Bamboo is way ahead of mere humans at taking the time to build an infrastructure and getting ready to be functional and beautiful.

This should be a lesson to all of us who will never see our twenties or thirties again. The early years were like the time the bamboo sat passively in the water, waiting for the growth spurt. That was when we got the tools together to be ready when the time is right. It's never too late to begin again.

To be happy, fulfilled and in control, we have to feel good about who we are and what we do. As children, we dreamed big dreams and knew no limitations. Over time, our parents, teachers and others around us generously informed us of our shortcomings, criticized our actions, and imposed their definition of success upon us. As adults, we replay these pre-recorded tapes over and over in our heads, doubting our ability and fearing the humiliation of failure and what others may think and say. We get a good education, spend years working hard for someone else, and eventually get good at something yet are unfulfilled and unhappy.

Make the decision today to build your belief and confidence in your ability. The internal growth process and belief system comes before the physical evidence. As you work on yourself, you'll accept responsibility for your future. Start by building your belief and confidence, knowing who you are, what you're good at and what brings you joy. The following exercises, stories and resources are all here to help you through this. It's a process that may happen quickly or may take some time, but you'll find your growth sudden and grand like those bamboo plants shooting up in growth spurts.

ARE YOU LETTING YOUR AGE OR CIRCUMSTANCES DEFINE YOU?

How about you? Have you got a dream you think will never happen because of who you are today and you've passed that time in your life? Nonsense! If you're breathing in and out, you can reshape your life. Nothing and no one can hold you back except yourself.

And don't try telling me you're too young or too old to change direction and turn your Power-Wants into reality. Maybe you saw the television movie *Homeless to Harvard*. It told the true story of Liz Murray who grew up without any of the basic comforts. Her father was gone, her mother was an addict, and Liz didn't have a permanent roof over her head for much of her young life. As a child, she was the adult in her dysfunctional family, but she was determined to get an education and go to a good school. Nothing stopped her and today she's at Harvard, not because she felt it was owed to her or because someone did her a favor. Liz Murray got there on her own, by her own dedication to her seemingly impossible vision of her future, which she formulated when, still a preteen.

And Liz isn't the only one to achieve this feat. Lauralee Summer did it too, graduating from Harvard after moving all around the country with her mother, living out of vermin-infested shelters and welfare hotels. When she was 12, her mother gave her up to foster care because she couldn't provide for the girl. Lauralee didn't meet her father until she was nineteen. After Harvard, she went on to graduate school at UC-Berkeley in California and her memoir, *Learning Joy from Dogs Without Collars,* was published in 2003. She is optimistic, loving, close to her mother and studying to give back to her community.

Liz Murray and Lauralee Summer prove you're never too young. You're never too disadvantaged. You're never helpless or hopeless. Liz and Lauralee wouldn't accept those excuses — and neither should you.

And if you're still not convinced, this story came over the Internet.

Rose was an 88-year-old college student, full of fun, loved and appreciated by her decades-younger classmates. When asked to address the Gridiron Banquet, she gave the following speech.

"You've got to have a dream. When you lose your dreams, you die. We have so many people walking around who are dead and don't even know it! There is a huge difference between growing older and growing up. If you are nineteen years old and lie in bed for one full year and don't do one productive thing, you will turn twenty years old. If I am eighty-seven years old and stay in bed for a year and never do anything I will turn eighty-eight. Anybody can grow older. That doesn't take any talent or ability. The idea is to grow up by always finding the opportunity in change. Have no regrets. The elderly usually don't have regrets for what we did, but rather for things we did not do. The only people who fear death are those with regrets."

Words for all of us to remember. Incidentally, Rose died in her sleep a few weeks after she graduated. Was her time and effort wasted? No. Almost 6,000 young friends attended her funeral, all profoundly influenced by her in one way or another. She had lived her life to the fullest and took joy in fulfilling her dream. Now, what's your excuse?

I hope Rose's story has encouraged you to get off the couch and start figuring out what your dreams are. As I see it, you have two options. You can sit and do nothing … or you can get up and make some changes. Whichever you do, the years will still pass. The question is, will you enjoy them? Do you want the next five years to look like the last five?

WRITING DOWN WHAT YOU WANT

It's time to begin identifying your dreams. If you're very lucky, you already know exactly what you want. Write it on the first line of Exercise # 6.

If you're like most of us, you have suppressed those dreams so long you need to be reminded. I've added some suggestions and hot buttons to get you started. Take a few minutes and write what would please you in the following parts of your life. You can leave blank any areas in which you are currently satisfied.

Don't worry if your dreams — which will soon become Power-Wants — seem out of reach. Write as much as you can as fast as you can. You can make them come true. Trust me — and more important, trust YOU!

Suggested Resources:

Books:

Learning Joy from Dogs without Collars by Lauralee Summers. (Simon & Schuster: 2003 — ISBN: 0743201027)

Ordinary Women, Extraordinary Lives by Marcia Chellis, (Penguin Books: 1992 — ISBN: 0-670-83757-1)

The Complete Idiot's Guide to Reinventing Yourself by Jeff Davidson. (Alpha Books: 2001. ISBN: 002864005.5)

Write It Down, Make It Happen: Knowing What You Want and Getting It! by Henriette Anne Klauser, Ph.D. (Simon & Schuster: 2000 — ISBN 0-684-8500I-X)

FIVE-MINUTE EXERCISE #6

I know what I want is to _____

_____

_____

_____

_____

My personal fitness dream (weight, exercise) is to _____

_____

_____

_____

My personal inner life dream (overcome shyness, anger, low self-esteem) is to

_____

_____

_____

_____

_____

My personal living dream (house, car, neighborhood) is to _____

_____

_____

_____

_____

_____

My personal career dream (job, company, future title) is to_____

_____

_____

_____

_____

My personal financial dream (salary, investments, savings) is to _____

_____

_____

_____

_____

My personal relationship dream (family, mate, children) is to_____

_____

_____

_____

_____

My personal perfect life dream (what would make me truly happy) is to __

_____

_____

_____

_____

ᏺ CHAPTER SEVEN ᏺ

"Soon," "Someday" and
"Eventually" Aren't on the Calendar

I don't need time, I need a deadline.
–Duke Ellington

A DREAM WITH A DEADLINE

The great jazz pianist was right. His words are echoed by motivational gurus who constantly remind us, "A goal is a dream with a deadline." I can relate to that, can't you? Just when we think we can't squeeze another hour out of our day, a crisis hits and there's something that needs to get done NOW. Ask any mother who is told at bedtime that she's been volunteered to bake three dozen cupcakes- and by the way, they're due the next morning. A deadline makes the impossible doable, even if it means an early morning visit to the bakery.

Another line I heard all the time when I was working in the corporate environment was, "There's never time to do it right, but there's always time to do it over." That's a trap we don't want to fall into. While it may work (more or less) in large companies, albeit with a load of grumbling by the poor souls assigned the redo task, it doesn't work at all outside the office. Unwise personal decisions made in haste can take years to undo and sometimes negatively impact the rest of our life.

What we think we want today might be the opposite of what we know we want tomorrow. That's why we want to take the time to be sure we're on the right track — and just as important, be ready to nip and tuck and alter that dream when it looks as if we're changing your direction.

You'll learn as you work on one goal that another may seem more or less important. Be flexible. There's no shame in changing your mind.

Sissy wanted to move out of Manhattan and live in the rural suburbs where she and her family could lead a stress-free life without cars and smog and crime and noise and people. She and Fred moved their three young children to a charming farmhouse in a far suburb on Long Island.

Although Fred had a two-hour commute each way, country living was going to be great. Sissy started a garden and planted all kinds of vegetables, but she couldn't stay ahead of the onslaught by rabbits and deer, creatures she'd never dealt with in the city. Most of her day was spent ferrying her children to various activities too far from the house for them to reach on foot. Even the most rudimentary grocery store was a 15-minute drive. The phones went out regularly, as did the electricity. As for luncheons with friends while the kids were in school, forget it. There were few restaurants open in that rural community and Sissy had no friends to be with and little chance to meet them. But it was quiet with few cars, clean air, no crime, no noise and no people. For Sissy and her family that meant it was boring.

After a year, Sissy was more stressed than she ever remembered being. Six months after that, to everyone's relief, they moved back to New York, this time finding a home in a gentrified section of Brooklyn where they were less pressured than in Manhattan, but still close enough to enjoy all the city had to offer. "Sometimes a dream becomes a nightmare," Sissy says. "That's when it's time to wake-up and get a new perspective."

Our dreams, like our calendars, clothes, and to-do lists, are in constant flux. The goal may stay the same while the details change, or the goal itself may morph into a different design than we originally imagined.

Sounds contradictory, doesn't it? Be careful what you want because you might get it, like Sissy and her family. Choose your goal thoughtfully and wisely. At the same time, be prepared to adjust your dream as you go along.

Actually, it makes a lot of sense. We want to consider our goals carefully. That puts us on the track. How we achieve the goals may change. Sissy and Fred's goal of living a less urban lifestyle never changed. By moving back to New York but staying out of Manhattan, they accomplished their dream in a way less stressful than their first path. It's okay to nip, tuck, tailor, lengthen, shorten and otherwise alter our dreams however we want. They're our private property to improve however we see fit.

In Five-Minute Exercise #7, pick one of your goals and think about how attaining it will change your life. Say you dream of adding an extra $1000 a month to your income. What changes would that make in how you live, dress, entertain, shop — think of all the ways your existence would be different. Don't forget what you would do for vacations or if you would change your car or your house. Try and be as detailed as possible about the ways in which attaining your dream will affect how you live.

You may be wondering why I want you to do this exercise. One of the things that keeps us from achieving our goals is that we aren't prepared for the life changes they will trigger. We read about the lottery winners who spend every penny and go back to being poor. The actual statistic is that 80% of lottery winners lose it all within two years.

Why? Obviously, they were unwise in how they managed their money, but the theme that emerges time after time is that they were unprepared for what the fortune did to them. They felt uncomfortable around old friends. They felt obligated to pick up the tab when they joined others for a dinner out. Their social circle began to change. They thought people expected them to dress and act differently. As a result of their discomfort, they unconsciously undermined their good fortune, emptied their bank accounts, and got back to their old secure world.

In a similar situation, Marsha had been overweight most of her life. When she finally lost almost one hundred pounds, she was amazed by the attention her new face and figure attracted. People, noticing her change of attitude as much as her new look, began to invite her to parties. She bought a new pretty wardrobe. Her social calendar filled up and men asked her out. Instead of being pleased, Marsha was frightened because she hadn't thought past the actual weight loss. Before long, she began putting on weight again and within a year was back to her old size and comfort zone.

Have you ever seen the ABC television program, *Extreme Makeovers?* Individuals are completely altered physically — breast implants, face lifts, nose jobs, tummy tucks, liposuction, laser eye surgery, dental implants -the works. They look incredible, hardly recognizable to their friends and family. Then they did a program that was a six-month follow-up on one of the extreme makeover recipients. Her friends were intimidated by her new looks. Some were jealous of her new sense of confidence and now found her arrogant, self-absorbed and distracted by the constant attention she received. They felt she was not the same person and no longer enjoyed her company.

That's why it's so important that you spend enough time thinking about what your existence will become with your new money or figure or education or residence, whatever your dream is. When you know what to expect, you can savor every moment of your success instead of fearing the unknown and ultimately failing.

Understanding the changes that lie ahead will also make you anticipate them more fully and want them all that much more. A true Power-Want is one you understand fully- from the initial striving for it to the final achievement. You know what it's going to take to reach it, and you're willing and eager to start the new life experience.

Suggested Resources:

Books:
Take Back Your Life: Smart Ways to Simplify Daily Life by Odette Pollar (Conart Press: 1999 — ISBN: 1-57324-132-6)

Time Management from the Inside Out: The Foolproof System for Taking Control of Your Schedule and Your Life by Julie Morgenstern. (Henry Holt: 2000 — ISBN: 0805064699)

Movie:
About Schmidt, Warren Schmidt (Jack Nicholson) has arrived at several of life's crossroads all at the same time. (2002 New Line Cinema Production)

FIVE-MINUTE EXERCISE #7
When I achieve my goal to _____, my life will change in the following ways: _____

_____

_____

_____

_____

_____

𝕮𝕨̇ CHAPTER EIGHT 𝕩̇

Signs along the Road to Success

> *It's not so much how busy you are, but why you are busy.*
> *The bee is praised; the mosquito is swatted.*
> *—Marie O'Connor*

WHERE THERE'S A WILL, THERE'S A WAY

There are as many ways to make money as there are people. The secret is to find something that will interest you and keep you moving forward toward your goal.

We are all familiar with **"working hard,"** doing something that earns us an income and getting paid (meagerly) for the job we do. Certainly if there was a way you could work one year and get paid for your work, not just for the year you worked but for the following year and the year after that, all without doing anything more, you would want to know about it. This is called **"Working Smart."** In the chapters ahead, we'll explain ways to generate passive, residual income. But first, let's look at some of the other ways people have made money.

Alison is a very accomplished photographer whose work hung in art galleries. Even though she was highly respected by other professional photographers, she's shy and hated the glad-handing that went along with being successful.

In order to find something that would support her so she could use her photography just as a hobby, Alison started a recycling business. She contacted the businesses in town and offered to buy their empty printer cartridges for $1 each. She then turns around and sells them to recyclers for

$4 to $5 each. Today, she's making $3,000–$5,000 a month for about 15 hours of work.

What Alison does takes no talent, no skill, and no training. What it takes is the ability to see a need and the willingness to fill it.

Obviously, I don't have the knowledge to talk about all the ways you can earn money, but Alison is a good example of how simple it can be.

If you're computer savvy, the Internet has turned the whole world into our marketplace. What might be considered commonplace in the United States is a treasure in Nepal. The audience is unlimited and if you exercise common sense, you'll be able to realize a nice profit for very little actual work.

Many people are using eBay.com and similar sites to sell everything from combs to cars at a profit. If you enjoy going to yard sales, you can pick up interesting items for a few dollars that will be prized by a buyer on the other side of the country — or the world. Amazon.com has a very active group of individuals who are selling their used books through the site. Or if you have a favorite family recipe or a needlework pattern, it can be sold on your own inexpensive website which you can set up and maintain for a few dollars a month. (Remember my earlier advice about computers … find a teenager! Check with your local high school computer teacher and see if he or she can recommend someone to help you for a very modest fee — or maybe even for class credit!)

You'll find several books on how to sell on the Internet successfully at any bookstore, or go on Amazon.com and look under the used books to buy them at a huge discount.

Edna was an expert knitter and friends were always asking her for patterns. Finally, she put her best patterns together in a brochure. Her neighbor's teenage son was happy to help her get a simple three page website up and she followed instructions on how to get it listed on the search engines.

She made the arrangements to take credit cards so she was paid before the brochure was sent out.

She offered the brochure for sale at $5 each, available either by mail or as a computer file. So far she's sold over 10,000 of the first brochure and has three more listed that are selling just as briskly.

* * * * * * * * *

Cindy wasn't a writer but she had an idea for a book. She called it *Everything Men Know About Women,* and had an interesting cover designed and a local printing company made up the books, which were filled with blank paper. She and her husband started advertising in local newspapers. Word spread and they sold over one million dollars worth of the books.

Today, Cindy lives in the house she always dreamed of and continues to publish simple books that people buy by the thousands.

* * * * * * * * *

Gracie had married right after high school and worked while her husband went to college and graduate school. She put off children during her twenties and in her thirties she couldn't conceive. At 38, her husband left her for his much-younger secretary.

Gracie was alone, had no money, and had been diagnosed with an auto-immune condition that would severely hamper her mobility within a few years. Because she had so little formal education, she had very few skills but she knew how to keep house and had demanding standards.

She started small putting notes up on the grocery store bulletin boards saying she was available for those who wanted outstanding cleaning services. Slowly her business grew and she hired and trained others. Within a couple years, Gracie ran the company from her home, keeping close tabs on her remarkably capable and loyal staff.

Most women who've found great success have found a real need that every one else had overlooked — and then they filled it.

Lane Nemeth started her home-based business out of her garage in Martinez, California. When her first child was born, Lane realized that high quality developmental toys weren't available commercially. Her background included a degree in design and time working in a day care center. This helped her develop her company, Discovery Toys.

The company had a two-fold mission: to provide educational products that develop life skills and encourage positive interaction between parents and children, and to provide a lucrative career opportunity to parents who sought the kind of flexibility that would allow them to stay at home with their children.

Today, Discovery Toys is a major, well-respected direct marketing company based in Livermore, California, where it occupies a large building housing the corporate offices, distribution and service centers.

* * * * * * * * *

Mary Kay Ash started out as a door-to-door distributor. She had gone to work as a young child after her father became ill and her mother worked 14 hours a day to try and support the family. In 1963, she was a single mother. With $5,000, she founded Mary Kay Cosmetics in a Dallas storefront. The firm sold products door to door using nine saleswomen, called "beauty consultants."

Thanks to Mary Kay's positive philosophy and her generous incentives for successful salespeople, the business grew steadily. Her representatives worked hard to earn their free pink Cadillacs, diamond jewelry and the respect of their leader. With over 300,000 sales people and more than $1 billion in sales from 19 countries, the firm remains a major presence in the competitive beauty market.

* * * * * * * * *

Lillian Vernon was born in Germany and fled to the United States shortly before the start of World War II. When she married in 1951, the couple received $2000 in cash. Lillian placed an ad in *Seventeen Magazine* to sell a personalized belt and purse. The ad cost $495 and within two weeks $32,000 in orders had been placed and a business was launched. Today, she runs Lillian Vernon Corporation, a specialty catalog company that fills more than five million orders a year for gift, household, gardening, decorative, and children's products.

What did these women have that most people don't have? They had incredible determination, tenacity, and focus on their goal to succeed. They allowed nothing to hold them back. They didn't accept the idea of limitation. They didn't worry about their education or lack of experience. When they needed to know something, they either took a class or found someone to do it for them.

THINKING OUTSIDE THE BOX

In the next exercise, think outside the box. Put your mind in overdrive and mentally skim through your day.

- What frustrates you?
- What do you see each day that needs to be fixed?
- What tasks take you longer because something isn't available that would make life so much easier?

- What service could someone provide for you that would greatly simplify your existence?
- What would help your kids learn?
- What would assist your elderly parents or grandparents with their decreasing mobility?
- What makes you laugh that would make others laugh too?

Don't worry about whether it's feasible or doable or rational. It might be an idea so way out that it defies logic, but maybe there's a way around the problems and a new product to be born. Pay attention to your internal signaling system, your gut feelings or hunches. We have all had them. They act as a traffic signal does, using an alternative source of power that gives you a sense that you should move forward, proceed with caution or stop! Think back to when you had a strong gut feeling. What decision did you make? What was the result? In the mid-1800s a housewife, angry that so many plates were chipped and broken while her maid cleaned up after meals, invented the dishwasher. The best business minds told her it would never be a product people would buy. Aren't we glad she didn't pay any attention to the so-called experts?

Just think of what you would like to have in a perfect world.

Correction fluid was invented by Betty Clair Nesmith whose grandson needed to correct a mistake he had made in his homework. She used a little of the white paint that was meant for the living room wall, daubing it on his paper and allowing it to dry so he could write over it. She didn't stop to think if it would work. She just found a need and tried to fix it. She went on to start and run the Liquid Paper company.

* * * * * * * * *

It was also a woman who invented the potato chip bag we take for granted today. Laura Scudder realized that the old method of scooping chips from a barrel into a paper sack meant lots of broken chips. So she ironed wax paper on three sides to make a bag and then ironed the top to seal it. Again, she saw a need and filled it.

* * * * * * * * *

So did Rommy Revson. In 1987, after a nasty divorce from Revlon cosmetics heir, John Revson, she had to find a job to support herself. To look her best, she bleached her hair, which started coming out in handfuls. She couldn't pull it back in a pony tail because the rubber band broke her brittle hair, so she invented an elastic band covered with soft fabric and named it after her dog, Scünci. Instead of going to work for someone else, she patented her idea, called it a "scrunchie," and, as of 2002, has sold over two billion of them. It sure beat working for someone else.

Keep coming back to Exercise #8 as new ideas hit you. You want to write them down or you'll forget them — until the day you realize someone else had the same idea but they moved ahead with it. (I have a friend who still has her business plan for a 24-hour store that would offer small business people duplicators and typewriters they could use rather than making the capital investment in equipment. She sent the idea to IBM. They said, "Thank you but no thank you, it won't work," so she dropped it. Within two years, a man across the country in California opened the first Kinko's. She's still kicking herself.)

Suggested Resources:

Books:

eBay for Dummies, 3rd Edition by Marsha Collier, Roland Woerner, Stephanie Becker. (Hungry Minds, 2002 — ISBN: 0764516426)

Home-Based Business for Dummies by Paul Edwards, Sarah Edwards, Peter Economy. (For Dummies: 2000 — ISBN: 0764552279)

Magazines:

Home Based Business — Quarterly subscription newspaper published by the National Association of Home Based Businesses (PO Box 10023, Rockville, *MD 20849 Fax: 301-963-7042 email: nahbb@crosslink.net.*

FIVE-MINUTE EXERCISE # 8

In a perfect world, I would like to have: _____

_____

_____

_____

_____

_____

_____

_____

_____

_____

In a perfect world, we would be able to: _____

_____

_____

_____

_____

_____

_____

_____

In a perfect world, I would like to see: _____

_____

_____

_____

_____

_____

_____

_____

_____

_____

_____

_____

_____

_____

❦ CHAPTER NINE ❧

Uncover Your Brilliance

> *The only place success comes before work*
> *is in the dictionary.*
> *—May V. Smith*

GET REAL

You've got it figured it out by this time. You need to make money if you're going to achieve any dream. If you examine your unachieved goals up to this point, how many of them would you have fulfilled if you could have afforded it? Probably several. So let's start thinking about how we're going to add those hundreds or thousands of dollars to your bank account every month.

First of all, let's debunk another old adage we hear all the time. We're always told: "You can be anything you want to be!" Not really.

If you're a petite blonde living in Idaho, I'm pretty sure you'll never be a sumo wrestler, no matter how much you might want it. You live in the wrong place, you're the wrong gender and you don't meet the size requirements. All the wishing in the world on your part isn't going to make it come true.

If you're six feet tall, you'll never be a competitive jockey. You might ride a horse, but you'll never measure up to a five-foot-two, one hundred and ten pound professional racecourse rider.

If you can't carry a tune and have no sense of rhythm, you'll never be a great musician. If you can't draw a straight line with a ruler, don't bother trying to be a great artist. These can be fun hobbies, but they won't make you your fortune.

You get the idea. There are some things that, no matter how much we want them, are never going to happen. So why butt your head against a brick wall when all you'll come away with is a bad headache? It makes more sense to find out what your skills, talents and passions are and use them to reach your goals.

K.D. Sullivan is the owner of a successful San Francisco proofreading and editorial services company. She doesn't have a college degree. In fact, she doesn't have her high school degree. She married young and by the time her son was a toddler, she was divorced, looking for a way to support the two of them without leaving the house. Examining her strengths, she realized that she had always paid great attention to detail. It disturbed her when things were out of order or didn't follow a pattern. She noticed when newspaper facts were wrong or there were inconsistencies in the way information was presented. She had always been a good speller, so she was very aware of the frequent mistakes she saw in printed materials.

Being very detail oriented, she looked in the Yellow Pages to find a professional proofreader so she could learn what the work involved. There wasn't even a category. So K.D. contacted the Yellow Pages and talked them into establishing a listing and putting her in it, even though they said it was too late for that year's book. She wasn't going to let a technicality stop her. No one gets between K.D. and her goals.

She then read everything she could find on proofreading, practiced constantly, and began to establish herself as an expert. She called companies she felt might need her services and work began to trickle in. With each job, her confidence grew — and so did her client list. Her son had a stay-at-home mother, and she had a growing business.

Twenty years later, she's the author of *Go Ahead...Proof It!,* a best-selling book teaching others how to proofread and the coauthor of a book on English, *The Art of Styling Sentences,* with other titles on the way. Her company, Creative Solutions, now employs dozens of independent writers, editors and proofreaders who are assigned to clients across the country.

YOU'RE SITTING ON A GOLD MINE — YOU

What skill do you have that can be translated into money? No one skill is better than another. You should concentrate on what pleases you, what makes you wonderful and unique. You'll be happier and more productive doing something you enjoy. Everyone of us is a winner, with gifts and talents we can use to enrich our lives and others.

- Are you a people person who likes working with the public?
- Are you a visionary who enjoys supervising, leading, mentoring people?
- Do you prefer being left alone to work on projects?
- Are you a self-starter who doesn't need supervision?
- Are you most efficient when you have to report your progress regularly?
- Are you driven to serve humanity and help others?
- Do you have a knack for sales?
- Do you enjoy new products and introducing them to others?
- Are you musically oriented; do you enjoy composing, listening, teaching or evaluating music?
- Do you love dance, theatre and the arts?
- Are your passions travel or photography?
- Is customer service your specialty?
- Are you a natural problem solver?
- Would you rather lead or follow?
- Are you detail oriented?
- Are you technically oriented, always pulling things apart and putting them back together again?
- Do you enjoy space design, layout and planning?
- Do you hate working in offices?
- Do you enjoy spending all day on the computer?

These are some of the questions I want you to ask yourself so you begin to get a feel for what kind of work will best suit your personality and nature. It is always easier to work with the grain instead of against it. Go with the flow. Do what feels best and most natural and you'll succeed that much faster.

Now, let's explore some other abilities you might have that you never thought of as moneymakers:

- Can you sew? Knit? Crochet? Embroider?
- Are you a good cook? Do you like to entertain?
- Would you enjoy teaching others to cook or catering small gatherings or large events?
- Do you enjoy making scrapbooks and other craft projects?

- Do you have any secretarial training?
- Are you good with words, enjoy reading, writing, editing, reporting?
- Are you efficient at running errands?
- Are you a neat freak who loves to clean?
- Are you an organizational wizard?
- Do you enjoy taking care of children?
- Does the sight of a bare room inspire decorating ideas?
- Are you a natural green-thumb gardener?
- Do you have fun working with animals?
- Can you coach any sport?
- Are you physically or athletically oriented. Do you like sports, sports therapy, massage therapy?
- Do you enjoy the outdoors, nature?
- How are your driving skills?
- Do you have good handwriting or know calligraphy?

I've just skimmed the surface of some of the activities you probably do everyday that you can convert into money-making enterprises. The secret is to discover what you do well and either do it for other people or teach others how to do it.

Say your special talent is cooking. Mrs. Fields and Wally "Famous" Amos both made fortunes with family cookie recipes.

Do you make up wonderful children's stories? Let's not forget that J. K. Rowling, the author of the Harry Potter books, wrote the first volume sitting in her brother-in-law's coffee shop with her baby in the carriage next to her. She was an out-of-work single mother who desperately needed money. Today, less than ten years later, she's officially wealthier than the queen of England.

REPETITION, REPETITION, REPETITION

It can be done. Your skills can be converted into cash. But you have to be willing to develop a business template and stick to it. Some of the most innovative ideas have made fortunes because once the basic pattern was developed, no one ever deviated from it. It's a recipe, a success formula simply duplicated over and over again. This is especially apparent in franchises like McDonald's or Starbucks. No matter where you are in the world, these stores look alike, serve uniform food, and every employee follows the rules established when the business was first opened.

What can you do that can be easily duplicated? What product or service can you offer that people will continue to need? Ray Kroc was impressed with how consistent the original McDonald's hamburger was and how efficiently the operation ran. He knew people always need to eat, and he kept that consistency when he bought the tiny MacDonald's hamburger stand and developed it into a huge international franchise.

Look at stores like Gap or Target or Blockbusters. Every store in every city looks the same. They're set up on the same floor plan. You never have to go searching. If the item you're seeking was on the right hand wall in San Francisco, it'll be on that same wall in Chicago and New York. A simple idea repeated over and over again equals success.

A JOSIE "MUST DO"

Are you computer literate? If you're not, you have to be willing to learn or settle back and prepare to be left behind in the dust. In the 21st century, being comfortable on the computer is as essential as knowing how to type or answer the phone. Even restaurant servers use computers to input the customer orders. The dry cleaner clerk asks for your phone number so the computer can display your address. Virtually nothing is done without computer input.

If you don't understand the computer, start learning it today. If you don't have a computer or can't afford a teacher, find a 13-year-old and spend some time at the library. Teenagers can teach you more than most commercial courses because they consider a computer as common as a pencil — and just about as simple to use.

This isn't an option. It isn't a suggestion. It isn't advice. It's an order! No matter what your Power-Wants and personal Future Book look like, you'll have a tough time turning them into reality without being at least reasonably computer literate.

THE ANSWER MAY BE RIGHT UNDER YOUR NOSE

If you're wondering what you can possibly do with the skills you have or can learn quickly, look around you. Most great inventions happened because someone saw a need and figured out how to fill it.

As a child, Carly was constantly rearranging furniture around the house. After she received her degree in design, Carly worked long and hard for a design firm. After she got married and became a mother, she stopped working. Her three children and her husband were her priorities. However, they needed money and Carly was always looking for a way to balance family and finances.

Through a few contacts in the real estate market, she started a staging business on a part-time basis. She would "set the stage" in homes for sale, decorating them to be more enticing when people walked through. First, Carly consulted with realtors on how they could best present their homes to potential buyers, then for a fee she would place temporary home furnishings in empty houses to make them more attractive to the people walking through.

Today, she buys furniture from consignment centers and slightly damaged or discontinued decorative items from stores. She charges a fee for her design services, and then charges rental fees for the items she places in homes. When the house sells, the furniture goes back to her warehouse and she reuses it for the next job. What a great business!

How often have you said, "I wish someone could....." or "Wouldn't it be great if such-and-such were available" or "Why hasn't anyone ever invented ....?" We say it all the time. If you want it, need it or would like someone to do it for you, then you can make it or do it for someone else. That may be your answer to a lifetime of financial security.

In Exercise #10, I want you to think about your special skills. What can you do better than all your friends? This is no time to be modest. After you make your list, number the skills beginning with the thing you would most like to do on a full-time basis. (Remember, you can always change your mind later.)

Also, begin thinking about things you wish had been invented because they would make your life easier. If you want or need the item, most likely someone else does too. There's your opportunity to come up with a new product that can make you money for the future.

As you do the exercise, ask yourself: "What would I do if I could be certain it would be a success? What would I do if I knew from the start there was no way I would fail?"

Most great ideas generated laughter at first and scoffers tried to diminish them. The successful people refused to listen to the critics and followed their hearts.

Every one of us is a winner. We possess special talents and gifts which we can use to fulfill our lives and enhance the world around us. We can compliment our lives by meeting and working with others who possess the skills and talents we are not as strong in and through that synergism create something even bigger than we could on our own.

Those who work in careers that fit their personalities and talents are much more fulfilled with their work, productive and happier. Those who do work that does not compliment or utilize their talents always feel a sense of longing for something else and never feel satisfied or fulfilled.

Look at the following talents people possess and determine where you shine. Think of ways you can develop your talent and use it to serve others through some business venture. Is there a way you can duplicate this process thereby multiplying your efforts and income and ultimately achieve your goals?

EVALUATE YOUR SKILLS:
Taken from Centers of Brilliance By Larry Koenig, Ph.D.

Words: You do very well working with words (writer, journalist, lawyer, secretary, English teacher, announcer, speech pathologist, translator, editor).

Logic: People good at working with numbers, matters of logic, creating hypotheses, thinking in terms of cause and effect and patterns or concepts. (estimating, auditing, accounting, systematizing, doing research , economic theory, budgeting, using statistics)

Picture/Spatial: You are good at transforming ideas into pictures and at conceptualizing three-dimensional space. (designing, inventing, mapping, photographing, decorating, drafting, illustrating, drawing, painting, teaching art, choreography, creating ads, visual presentations, filming or visualizing)

Body Brilliance: People who are gifted do well at using their body. Skilled at physical movements, handling objects and eye-hand coordination.

Happiest while organizing or playing sports, modeling, acting, performing, installing, repairing, restoring, wood working, building, miming, dancing, manufacturing, delivering, working outside.

Emotional and Spiritual: People are good at knowing the inner self, both theirs and other, they excel in spiritual and philosophical thought, are introspective and tuned into feelings of those around them. (counseling, helping others, writing, planning and organizing, problem solving setting goals, meditating, discerning opportunities, appraising or evaluating and working alone)

Musical: These people are happiest and excel when engaged in singing, playing instruments, composing, arranging music, conducting, teaching music, directing, analyzing and evaluating, transcribing music.

People: You have a unique ability to perceive the moods, intentions, emotions, and personalities, motivations and desires of other people. Excel at empathizing, tutoring, counseling, selling, coaching, coordinating activities, assessing others, teaching, leading seminars, persuading, motivating, recruiting, inspiring, encouraging, supervising, collaborating, leading teams, negotiating, mentoring and publicizing.

Suggested Resources:

Books:

Do What You Love and the Money Will Follow, Discovering Your Right Livelihood by Marsha Sinetar. (DTP, Reissue ed.: 1989 ISBN: 0440501601)

A Millionaire's Notebook: How Ordinary People Can Achieve Extraordinary Success by Steven K. Scott (Fireside: 1996 — ISBN: 0684803038)

What Color Is Your Parachute? 2004: A Practical Manual for Job-Hunters and Career Seekers, by Richard Nelson Bolles. (Ten Speed Press: 2003 — ISBN: 1580085415)

Movie:

Seabiscuit; Universal Pictures 2003 with Jeff Bridges. An American epic of triumph and perseverance.

FIVE-MINUTE EXERCISE #9

Skills I am noted for are: _____

_____

_____

_____

Hobbies I am good at are: _____

_____

_____

_____

_____

Training I've had includes: _____

_____

_____

_____

_____

_____

I would hire me to: _____

_____

_____

_____

_____

_____

I wish someone would invent a _____

_____

_____

_____

_____

_____

_____

_____

_____

🎇 CHAPTER TEN 🎇

Ask and the Universe Will Answer

> *You don't need energy suckers in your life. Accent the positive; elimi-*
> *nate the negative. That includes people, places and things.*
> *–Dr. Judith Briles*

YOUR POWER IS IN YOUR ATTITUDE

This is a very touchy subject with some people because it asks you to make some hard decisions. Nothing positive is going to happen in your life if you surround yourself with negative people and live in negative atmospheres. In the 1950s, Earl Nightingale said, "We become what we think about."

He went on to say that the idea, which he called "The Strangest Secret," wasn't original with him. He'd read the same thought expressed by dozens of authors since the beginning of recorded time. It can even be found in the Old Testament: "…as a man thinketh in his heart, so is he." (Proverbs 23:7)

The point is — if we think about being poor, we're going to be poor. If we think about being miserable and sick and discouraged, that's exactly how we're going to wake up every morning and go to bed every night. But if we think of ourselves as vibrant and healthy, with plenty of money, living where we want to live and doing what we want to do, our subconscious mind will help us make that picture a positive reality.

YOUR RETICULAR ACTIVATING SYSTEM

Thousands of sensory messages are constantly bombarding your brain. If they all got through, we would be unable to function because we'd be in sensory overload and couldn't process the information. Luckily there is a group of cells, about the size of a little finger, located at the base of the brain stem. This is the Reticular Activating System or RAS and it acts as a filter system for your brain, alerting or arousing you to what's important and storing the rest in your subconscious. The only information that it allows through to your consciousness is what you have decided is important to you or a threat to your welfare.

When you're achieving goals, the RAS roars into action, pulling information from the subconscious and alerting our conscious brain about things that will help us. You've already experienced it. We all have.

Say you decide to buy a yellow convertible VW Bug. I guarantee that once you make up your mind you'll see yellow convertible VW Bugs everywhere you go. They'll be next to you in the parking lot, ahead of you at the light, in the movie you watch on cable. Even if you had never thought about a yellow convertible VW Bug before, once you decide you want one the Reticular Activating System in your brain will point them out to you constantly.

Be aware of what is happening around you and notice the people you are meeting. Once you make a decision about what you want and start down the path of success all sorts of new people will come into your life. We have all said or heard someone say, "Isn't that a coincidence?" What you think of as coincidences, serendipitous or synchronistic events, are really the "signs" of success.

A study involved two pianos at opposite ends of a room. When a note was struck on one piano, the same note vibrated on the piano across the room. Like the piano strings, we also send off vibrations, which may be why we refer to people as having "good vibes." With these vibrations, you'll find yourself attracting others of the same mindset and they will be attracted to you. The Law of Attraction responds to your thoughts or vibrations, positive or negative, intended or unintended.

The opposite effect happens when you decide not to think about something. If I tell you not to think about pink elephants — and especially if I show you a picture of the elephant while I tell you you're forbidden to think about it — it will be almost impossible for you to obey me. Your RAS would keep bringing pink elephants to your consciousness. This is the reason all affirmations are positive statements.

- *I am a neat and tidy person.*
- *I can pass the test.*
- *I see myself as thin and healthy.*
- *I can have money in abundance.*

The RAS is also why so many times diets don't work. We fixate on what we won't eat and that's all we think about. Or if you say a negative affirmation — the picture your RAS will keep in the forefront of your brain are cigarettes and the cravings will be harder to resist.

The answer is to put your Reticular Activating System to work when you want to lose weight and only think of how wonderful you will look without the extra pounds and how healthy and fit you will be after all that exercise. To quit smoking, think about how sweet your clothes will smell and how healthy your lungs will be when they're smoke free.

The two things you must be certain to provide are a very specific goal and the personal accountability to react to the messages you're receiving. With those factors in place, your Reticular Activating System will help you make your vision become reality.

Here's a story I can guarantee is true because it's my own. In 1993, I was pregnant and my husband Joe and I lived in a house with my mother and brother in Sunnyvale, California, southeast of San Francisco. We wanted our own space for our family, so we started putting down on paper what we considered our wish list.

We needed two houses — or at least a duplex — because we have my mother to care for. We wanted a corner lot because they are usually larger, and we wanted to be near a library. (Mother always spoke highly of my cousins who lived next to a library and were so smart because they spent all their time there.)

We also wanted to be near a park so our children wouldn't have to cross busy streets to play — the way my brother and I had. Joe wanted a detached garage. We needed to stay in Mountain View or Sunnyvale so my aging mother would be close to relatives, friends and her church. What's more, whatever we found had to be under $300,000.

Debbie, who was one of the most successful real estate agents in the country for her firm, politely informed us that our wish list of seven very specific requirements was somewhat impossible. Housing in the Bay Area started higher than our limit. At the time, duplexes were selling for $400,000 or more. We continued to look somehow knowing that we would find an answer.

Joe spent a lot of hours driving around the two cities and then he spotted two abandoned homes on a corner lot, with a detached garage, next to a library, down the street from a park. No kidding! Two months after that, the city of Mountain View advertised they were auctioning off homes and the two Joe had found were listed. We agonized for weeks over the bid amount and were the highest of fourteen bidders, finally getting the houses for $295,000. Imagine if we had believed our agent when she said, "It can't be done."

Even better, five years later we sold this property for $750,000 and bought our first million dollar home.

Most people would say we just got lucky. Most say, "you were at the right place at the right time. That can't happen for me," or "for sure it can't happen again."

I don't think luck, in the normal sense, had very much to do with it. Instead I agree with the motivational speakers who say luck happens when preparation meets opportunity. That means good fortune doesn't drop into your lap. You have to be looking for and able to recognize the brass ring when it comes your way — and willing to do whatever it takes to grab the prize and make it work for you.

Joe and I had a plan, a dream, a vision. We took the time to write down the specifics of what we wanted knowing that this would best serve our family and because we refused to let anyone steer us away from that goal, we were persistent about what we wanted and kept patient and focused, maintaining strong feelings of belief until we found the perfect match and our vision came true. Most of us find ourselves where other people want us to be. We're the victims of other people's plans for us, which is the same as saying we're the victims of our own lack of planning for ourselves.

THE I-DON'T-CARE ATTITUDE TOWARD OTHER PEOPLE'S PESSIMISM

All the planning in the world will do you no good at all if you let other people's pessimism drive you away from your goal. You need to be totally confident in yourself, no matter how crazy someone says your idea is.

In 1944, scarlet fever and pneumonia left four-year-old Wilma Rudolph with one leg useless and in a brace. She didn't walk until she was seven years old. She was advised to rest her leg and find sedentary things to do. Instead, she became a high school athlete and when she became ill again at 18 and had surgery at 19, no one thought she would ever walk again.

They didn't know Wilma. She qualified for the 1960 Olympic team, winning the 100-meter dash and 200-meter dash during the Rome games. She was a member of the U.S. relay team that set a world record in the 100-meter dash at those games. In 1960, she was the first American woman runner to win three gold medals in a single Olympics.

For the next two years, she continued breaking her own records before retiring from competition, earning her college degree, and becoming the track coach for Tennessee State University.

If she had listened to the "wisdom of the day," Wilma Rudolph would have been a forgotten cripple. She had other plans for her life and she made them come true.

There is no way to over-emphasize the importance of listening only to your inner voice, your intuition, your gut feelings. It's vital that you stop to think about the people who drag you down or discourage you or make fun of you. Who are they? Do you need them in your life? If they are family or your spouse or children, you have to face them head-on and explain how you feel about their lack of respect for your plans. Try to get them to see your side. If they can't, then actively tune them out. We can't divorce our relatives but we can turn down their volume. Remote controls aren't the only things that come equipped with a mute button.

If you think it's impossible to ignore these people, remember how you ignored your parents when you were growing up. They had a lot to say, and you only listened to a small portion of it and probably didn't believe any of it. That's one teenage habit you need to cultivate again.

One woman confided to me that she had lots of dreams but her parents told her she shouldn't even try and reach them because she'd dropped out of college to marry and have children. "I don't have a bachelor's degree," she said sadly, "so who'll listen to me?" I reminded her that Bill Gates, the CEO of Microsoft and the richest man in America, doesn't have a college degree. If that's a problem, it's your problem, not his. If he could make it without college, what was holding her back? There's no blame in not knowing. The blame is only in refusing to learn.

I couldn't very well tell her to turn her back on her parents, but I certainly hope she found the strength to hit the mute button rather than listen to their negative and destructive comments. Just because we're related to people or because they're older aren't reasons enough to allow them to pour cold water on our dreams and goals.

So whether we're talking about friends or classmates or family or work associates, it's time to make some hard decisions. A real friend would be supportive. Anyone who tries to keep you from surpassing your potential doesn't belong in your address book. Surround yourself with upbeat, excited, positive people and you'll see how the goals you're reaching for become achievable.

WHAT'S YOUR SPIN?

Your bank balance is getting bigger. Your bills are getting smaller. You are beginning to see the light at the end of the tunnel. The pictures in your Future Book seem less out of reach. Everything is rosy. Life is good. But you're sure it's luck and it's not going to last because you don't deserve it. In other words, your attitude sorely needs an adjustment.

There is a dangerous enemy out there who is gunning for all of us. It's the worm of low self-esteem, that sneaky thought pattern that invades our thoughts, convincing us that we are silly to think we have a chance at success. The result is that we're cynical, depressed, not trusting our abilities. Instead of being upbeat and optimistic, we're waiting for the axe to fall, the other shoe to drop or for that light at the end of the tunnel to be a freight train heading in our direction.

Yes, that's an old joke, and I used it to remind you of a very important fact we talked about earlier. A large share of our most popular comedians get laughs by being pessimistic, cutting, cruel, and by tearing down the traditions we have all grown to accept. They delight in smashing icons and pulling people off pedestals, and we feed their fury by cheering them on.

It's only natural to repeat their best lines, and pretty soon we're sounding just as down-at-the-mouth as they do. But for them, it's an act. For us, it becomes part of our personalities, weighing us down. It's not so funny when you're the one being attacked — especially when you're attacking yourself.

Having an upbeat attitude about everything you do is as vital to your financial success as any college degree or lottery win or windfall inheritance. There's an anonymous bit of poetry that explains it pretty well:

If you think you're beaten, you are,
If you think that you dare not, you don't,
If you'd like to win, but you think you can't,
It's almost certain you won't.

But there's good news. There are many things in life we don't have much control over, but we can change our attitude. The bad news is, nobody can do it for us. As another anonymous poet said:

It's a beautiful world to see,
Or it's dismal in every zone,
The thing it must be in its gloom or its gleam
Depends on you alone.

It takes a desire to be an optimist and see the glass as half full instead of the pessimistic description of half empty. The public relations types call it "spin," putting everything in the best light possible. Here's how this works.

The Pessimist	**The Optimist**
It's rained for a week. I'm growing mold.	Isn't it great? No drought!
I've only sold one thing this week.	I sold one — it's starting to work!
I lost my job, now I'll starve.	I lost my job, now I can get a better one!
I broke my leg, I can't walk.	I broke my leg, it's good I can still talk!
I haven't lost a pound all week.	I haven't gained a pound all week!
I just don't know how.	I can find a way!
It's not my fault.	I can learn from this!
I don't know if I can do that.	I can commit to doing that!
That's the way it's been and will be.	We can find a better way to doing this!

Spins can be positive or negative. The news media loves the negative spin. "Ten people died in Monday's apartment house fire," the headline blares. That's sad, but just as important is that 80 walked away without a scratch.

Advertisers use positive spins all the time. "New and improved" is the positive spin on "It's better than the old one that didn't work so well."

You are in charge of putting the spin on your life. If you look at the positives instead of the negatives, you'll begin to see opportunities instead of barricades.

Josie's Advice to Negative People
SW. SW. SW? Next!
Some Will. Some Won't. So What? Next!

We know that a great many people are content to live mediocre lives, dissatisfied and defeated. Their attitude of negativity pours all over our bubbling enthusiasm in the hope of dampening our dreams. The second you hear or feel one bit of negativity from someone else, walk away or hang up and say to yourself, NEXT! Remember hearing "No" from someone simply means "No, not yet." or "No, I'm just not ready to hear your information." Focus on the people you need to meet to help you reach your goals and your RAS will bring them to you.

I want you to think about the people who may be holding you back. You have to identify them so you can be aware of their influence on you and begin to put them at arm's length or banish them from your life altogether.

A DIVINE PLAN

Each of us is a unique individual. There are no two sets of identical fingerprints. You have come into this world with your own special light and life. Some believe everything happens for a reason, some don't. There are people who believe in God, an Infinite Intelligence, a Higher Power — whatever name you choose to use — and there are those who don't. Personally, many things humble me, including people of great accomplishments, resounding beauty in art and music and the awesome wonders of nature. I feel we're all interconnected but operating independently to produce and provide for a greater purpose. As in an orchestra, each individual practices diligently and plays their part. There are highs and lows, loud booms and silence, and when everyone comes together we make incredible music. Although we may not understand it today, we will come to know our place in the bigger picture. To drudge through life, day after day, week after week, year after year, to make ends meet isn't serving yourself or the world around you well, let alone the Force that brought you here in the first place.

Nelson Mandela summed it up well in his 1994 inaugural speech: *We ask ourselves, who am I to be brilliant, gorgeous, talented, and fabulous? Actually, who are you not to be? You are a child of God. Your playing small doesn't serve the world…and as we let our own light shine, we unconsciously give other people permission to do the same.*

SORTING THE WHEAT FROM THE CHAFF

In Exercise #10 you're going to start identifying the people who are holding you back and what steps you're going to take to end their influence over you. You'll also name those in your list of friends who support and encourage you and decide what you can do to benefit from the gifts they offer you. In each case, it's the second step that's the hardest. We know who to avoid and who to embrace. It's more difficult to articulate how we will achieve what we want and when we are going to begin the process.

SUCCESS TECHNIQUE #2

This is a conditioning challenge.
Wear a rubber band around your wrist for two weeks. (Anything done for 30 straight days becomes a habit.) Every time you make a negative comment or have a negative thought, give yourself a snap with your rubber band. Immediately replace your negative thought with a positive thought. You can only hold one thought at a time and the more you condition yourself to think positively, the faster your dreams will come to fruition.

Suggested Resources:

Books:

The Confidence Factor: Cosmic Gooses Lay Golden Eggs, by Dr. Judith Briles (Mile High Press, 2001 — ISBN: 1885331045)

The Confident Woman by Marjorie Hansen Shaevitz (Harmony Books: 1999 — ISBN: 0609603523)

The Strangest Secret Revisited by Earl Nightingale (www.earl-nightingale.com)

Spontaneous Optimism: Proven Strategies for Health, Prosperity & Happiness by Dr. Michael W. Mercer and Dr. Maryann V. Troiani. Castlegate Publishers: 1998 — ISBN: 0938901095)

Success Through a Positive Mental Attitude by W. Clement Stone (Simon & Schuster; Reissue edition, 1992 — ISBN: 0671743228)

Song:

You Gotta Be (Sony 1994) by Des'ree

GIMME FIVE! EXERCISE # 10

The people who are holding me back with their negativity are: _____

_____

_____

_____

_____

_____

The steps I am going to take to change their influence on me are: _____

_____

_____

_____

_____

_____

_____

_____

The people who support and encourage me are: _____

_____

_____

_____

_____

_____

_____

These are the steps I'll to take to benefit more fully from their support: ___

_____

_____

_____

_____

_____

_____

_____

_____

_____

_____

_____

_____

_____

_____

_____

_____

THOUGHT PROVOKER – CHECK YOUR ATTITUDE
Here's a test of your attitude and optimism.
What do you see in the box below?

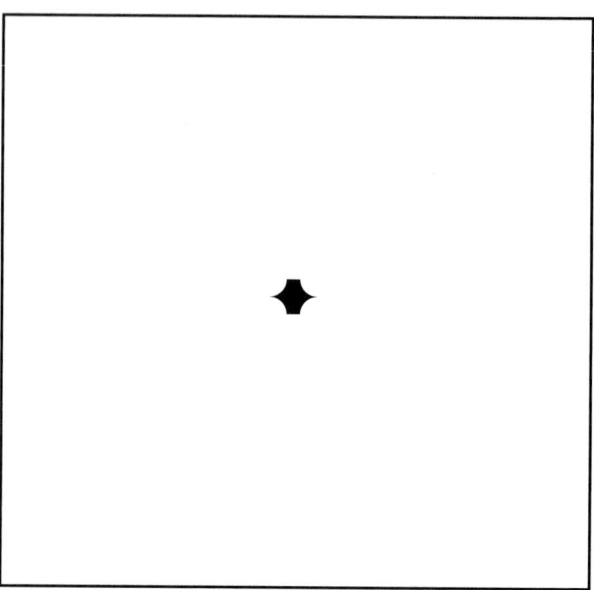

Do you see a large black design in the middle of a box?
Or do you see a huge white opportunity around a small black design?
Your future is what you imagine it to be — small and confined —
or huge and full of promise.

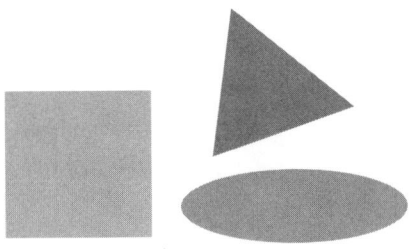

Section III:
Become Money-Smart

GIMME FIVE! RULE NUMBER THREE

"Use money as a tool and not as a prize, and it will build you a fortune."

⚙️ **CHAPTER ELEVEN** ☙

The Time and Money Relationship

> *"I believe one thing, that today is yesterday and tomorrow is today,*
> *and you can't stop."*
> *–Martha Graham*

THE MONEY MINT WE ALL HAVE

Each of us is given 24 hours a day — free of charge. That works out to 168 hours a week or about 720 hours in a 30-day month, or 8760 hours a year. If you work 40 hours a week, deduct 2080 hours a year. Let's say you sleep eight hours a night, which for most women is very generous; deduct another 2920 hours. Let's estimate another five hours a day for chores and entertainment, so we'll deduct 1825 hours. You have 1935 hours remaining each year.

That means you have about 5 hours a day or 150 hours a month that aren't accounted for. Maybe that doesn't sound like much, but what if you could charge $10 an hour for that time? That's an extra $1,500 a month. Charge $20 an hour and that's $3,000 a month going into your account.

Consider again: What did you say you would do if you had an extra $1000 a month?

Earl Nightingale, one of the 20th century pillars of self-development, said that each of us has a money-making machine under our roof but we don't think to turn it on. That machine doesn't print dollar bills. It spews out hours we can turn into cash.

Do, Delegate or Delete

Think about it. If you aren't working full-time at a job, you can add those hours to the pot. If you're spending hours doing chores, enlist the help of the other people in the household so you can free up time.

Look at the tasks at hand and decide to get them done, just do it or perhaps delegate.Can a friend, spouse, the kids or someone else handle it? Two loads of laundry may take an hour or two to wash, dry and fold, but the local laundry mat offers the service for $20.00 for two full loads. Now you have one hour to devote to your children, learning a new skill, exercising, gardening or getting to read the book that's been sitting on your nightstand for a month. Get rid of things that consume your time and don't enrich your life or move you toward your goals; throw out junk mail immediately, delete unsolicited emails and skip the nightly news.

Even young children can be taught to set the table, make their beds, pick up their clothes, and dust. Make it a game — or better yet, make it a paying job. It will teach them at an early age that work should be recompensed. Experts say that an allowance should be a gift but chores can be paid for. Just as important, teach them to save part of what they make and give part to charity. These will be tiny amounts of money to teach a huge life lesson.

If you live alone, decide to cut back on the housework. Washing the windows or cleaning out the closet won't make you money today. Learn how to do the necessary chores in the shortest time possible. A friend's mother calls it "give a flick and a promise." She means you flick the dust rag over the surface and promise to come back later for a more thorough job. Try it. It works.

I would bet you waste a lot of time each day. I know I used to — it's easy to do. Relaxation is important, but if you're using it to watch the third rerun of a television program you didn't much enjoy the first time, then you're throwing money out the window.

Objection: "I have no skills anyone would pay me for."

If your rationale for not being able to earn money is that you have no skills, think about this. It's been proven if you concentrate on learning a subject for an hour each day, you'll be an expert in the field within a year. Depending on its complexity, you'll probably be thoroughly competent to utilize your new skills much sooner than that. And all it takes is the investment of your formerly wasted time.

You'll find one hour a day if you really want to. Get up an hour earlier or go to bed later. Read only pertinent email messages. Immediately throw out junk mail and catalogues. Stop watching the late night news; instead read or listen to material that will help you develop yourself, your mindset and your new skill set.

I took a copperplate calligraphy class simply because I enjoy the hobby and the beauty of the end product. During one of the courses I discovered you can charge up to $1.00 per line for wedding invitations. Three lines at $1.00/line times 50 invitations equals $150.00 of additional income.

Objection: "I don't want to give up all my leisure time."

You don't have to give it all up — and you only have to give up some of it for a period of time. How strong is your WHY? A short-term sacrifice to yield you long-term stability and security is worth the price. Look at how much time is spent getting a higher education. We're happy to make the sacrifice to achieve a desired outcome.

When you have income coming in and feel comfortable personally and financially, you can cut back on the time you work. Of course, by then all your hour allocations will have changed. You probably won't be working 40 hours a week for someone else, because you'll have learned you can earn more being your own boss or you've learned to discipline yourself to live, save, and invest to meet the goals that will provide the lifestyle you want to live.

Objection: "I am too old to change the way I live."

Are you reading this book? That means you're alive- and that means you're not too old. They say you can't teach old dogs new tricks, but of course you can …as long as the dog is willing to learn!

The first lesson is how to most effectively use your time. To do that, you have to know what you're doing with it now. Lawyers keep track of their time in 15-minute increments and sometimes 10-minute segments. If a lawyer's time is billed out at $300 an hour and she spends ten minutes on the phone with you, you'll be billed for $50. Count on it!

Why is a lawyer's time any more important than yours? It isn't! Your time is worth whatever value you put on it. If $300 an hour sounds a bit high right now, let's say your time could bill out at $100 an hour. That means it costs you $50 to watch a sitcom. It costs you $100 to do the grocery shopping. An evening spent gossiping with friends is worth $400 of your time. (This doesn't mean you shouldn't enjoy yourself. You definitely should. But you should also know what it is really costing you. Make sure the fun you've planned is worth it.)

Consider this. If you're spending an afternoon going from store to store to find a bargain, it could be costing you $300 of your time to save $25 or $50. How much are you "spending" to save a few dollars?

From that perspective your time takes on a whole new meaning. If you get up at seven in the morning and go to bed at eleven at night, that's $1600 of time you've had at your disposal. How much of that did you just fritter away?

Again, don't become so fixated on the dollar value of each hour that you don't allow time for relaxation and fun. You can't perform at your best if you work all the time. We need some "down time." Take it and consider it "money" well spent.

Here's an example of how taking a rest can increase your effectiveness.

Two Oregon lumberjack teams were in a competition to see which team could cut the most wood in eight hours. Team One worked without stopping for the full time, amazing spectators with their strength and endurance.

Team Two worked two hours, then took a ten-minute break. Two hours later they took another break, and then did it again until their final 90 minute push. Everyone watched shaking their heads.

Who won? Team Two took the honors by a wide margin. You see, not only did they rest for a bit so they were refreshed, they used the rest time to re-sharpen their axes. It's a lesson for all of us. Are you taking the time to sharpen your axe?

Now that I've proved you've got to have some fun to be at your best, let's figure out where your time is going. Most diet gurus advise you keep a food diary to track what you actually eat in a day. My seminar students have found that keeping a Time Diary for a month makes them look at their lives in a whole new light. Many have been convinced by just a week's listings. On the next page is a sample you can either photocopy 30 times or copy into your own digital or paper notebook. If you want to be even more precise, any office supply store will have a professional calendar that breaks down the day into even smaller increments.

Whatever system you use, fill out the pages faithfully. Then add up what each activity "costs" you. You can set your personal hourly rate at any figure that feels comfortable to you, but don't underestimate your worth.

You can add up the money in several ways. If you're working eight hours, you don't have to count that time at all, or you can deduct what you make from whatever price per hour you feel you're worth. Remember, if you get a lunch hour during your workday, that hour could be spent working on your new skills so any other activity "costs" you.

Be honest with yourself. I guarantee you'll be amazed at how many hours you waste each day.

MY TIME DIARY

Day/Date: _____   I'm worth $/hour
AM

6:00 – 6:30	_____	$_____
7:00 – 7:30	_____	$_____
8:00 – 8:30	_____	$_____
9:00 – 9:30	_____	$_____
10:00 – 10:30	_____	$_____
11:00 – 11:30	_____	$_____

PM

12:00 – 12:30	_____	$_____
1:00 – 1:30	_____	$_____
2:00 – 2:30	_____	$_____
3:00 – 3:30	_____	$_____
4:00 – 4:30	_____	$_____
5:00 – 5:30	_____	$_____
6:00 – 6:30	_____	$_____
7:00 – 7:30	_____	$_____
8:00 – 8:30	_____	$_____
9:00 – 9:30	_____	$_____
10:00 – 10:30	_____	$_____
11:00 – 11:30	_____	$_____
12:00 – 12:30	_____	$_____

Once you've kept your Time Diary for a week, look it over closely. I'll bet you can pick out five hours you could redirect to activities that will make you money. If nothing else, you have those five lunch hours!

It's time to make goals you can accomplish in those five hours. If there's a book you need to read, spend five hours a week on it. If it takes you more than five hours to finish the book, that's fine. The point is you're meeting your goal of spending five hours a week on it.

In the same way, you can practice your typing skills, work on your business plan, look through magazines to find pictures of your dreams, read textbooks, take classes, practice your new activities….no matter what you want to do, five hours a week is plenty of time to start doing it. That's one hour a day, five days a week. How hard is that?

For Five-Minute Exercise #11, I want you to make a pact with yourself. This is a contract between the you who exists today and the you who's going to be in your skin tomorrow. It looks deceptively simple, but I want to take this as seriously as you would if you were signing a mortgage or a car loan. You are making a promise to yourself and you should be as strict about "payment" as the toughest lender.

Suggested Resources:

Books:

Time Management from the Inside Out: The Foolproof System for Taking Control of Your Schedule and Your Life by Julie Morgenstern (Henry Holt: 2000 — ISBN: 0805064699)

Checklists for Life: 104 Lists to Help You Get Organized, Save Time, and Unclutter Your Life by Kirsten M. Lagatree. (Random House: 2000 — ISBN: 0375707336)

How Smart Women Balance Family & Career, by Danielle Kennedy, (South-Western College Publishing, 2002 — ISBN 0324187505)

Website:

WorkingMom.com: The working mother's place for spiritual replenishment and help

FIVE-MINUTE EXERCISE #11

I, _____, hereby promise to spend not less than five hours each week in the pursuit of my dream to _____

_____

_____

_____

_____

_____

_____

_____

I will undertake the following activities during those five hours: _____

_____

_____

_____

_____

_____

_____

_____

_____

_____

_____

I will continue to meet this obligation towards my future until my vision has become a reality.

_____   _____

Signed: Date:

✥ CHAPTER TWELVE ✥

Solving the Money Mystery

> *"I don't know much about being a millionaire,*
> *but I bet I'd be darling at it."*
> *—Dorothy Parker*

WHAT DOES MONEY MEAN TO YOU?

You would think that money is money is money. No great mystery there. However, nothing could be farther from the truth. Each one of us looks at money a little differently. To some, it symbolizes power; to others freedom. Some people think of it as a means of buying happiness. Others consider it security. Where one person wants to amass as much as possible, someone else feels it's dirty and can't wait to give it away either to church or a charity or family members — or to department stores while trying to make herself happy.

Women can have a strange and often unhealthy relationship to money. If you're over 55, you may have been taught that women who talk about money aren't nice. Money wasn't discussed in that generation. Women were expected to have their husbands provide for them. If the woman worked, her salary went into the common pot so the man could make the decisions.

The Baby Boomers were a little more upfront about money, but it still wasn't considered important to teach girls how to handle their own finances. That generation began to see the rise of single mothers who had to be responsible but who didn't know they had the ability to alter their circumstances substantially.

Generation X, those who were born in the 1960s and 1970s, were the first group in which women routinely planned for their financial independence. But even then, many young women feel as if they're victims of circumstances.

Those who grew up at the end of the 20th Century, Generation Y, have even more choices. Young women are pursuing careers and putting off starting their family until they are in their thirties. Their relationships are partnerships, sharing responsibilities and decisions. In fact, there are more women in the workforce than ever, making more than ever and often exceeding their husband's or partner's income.

Whatever your age, I want you to be very sure of one thing: You can be in control of your financial security. It'll take work. It'll take effort. You'll be tired sometimes and you may doubt yourself sometimes, but I can promise you this: If you really follow the *Gimme Five!* Method, by this time next year you'll be in a better position financially than you've ever been before — and probably much sooner.

But before we start talking about how to make money, you've got to understand your relationship to it. Basically, money is like oxygen in that we need it to live. If we can't make our own oxygen, we end up on a machine that breathes for us at a tremendous cost. In the same way, when we have to depend on anyone else for our money, we do it at a tremendous cost. The only "free money" is what we earn for ourselves.

HOW TO BECOME WEALTHY

There are basically five ways we can become wealthy. Starting with the least likely, we can win the lottery — or we can marry into money, inherit it, earn it working for someone else or build it for ourselves.

The first four can be discounted as improbable, unlikely, unusual, or impossible. Why is it impossible to become wealthy working for someone else? Because whenever someone else signs your paycheck, there will be a limit on it. No matter how good you are at your job or how diligently you work or how much revenue you bring into the company coffers, you are dependent on someone else's generosity every time you get a paycheck. Furthermore, there's the chance those paychecks could end through no fault of yours.

The only valid path to wealth is to build your financial security by yourself. Studies of wealthy families show most of the money was made in one generation by people who started their own companies. Subsequent generations either maintained and grew the fortune — or most threw it away entirely by the third generation.

Remember, when you're building your own business, you have 100% of your attention working for you. No one else's interests have to be met. You can set up residual income producing businesses without anyone's permission. You don't have to answer to a board or stockholders. You have total flexibility and freedom, choices and opportunity.

But before you start planning how to begin building your own wealth, we have to clarify how you feel about the subject of money. Only when you can look at money as nothing more than an important and powerful tool — and not as a solution to your every problem — can you confidently begin to turn your life around.

In the next exercise, I want you to really understand your relationship to money. I've given you several choices as well as a space to write in anything I may have missed. Check off every answer that fits what money means to you — and then write the explanation next to it. For example, if money means freedom, write down what it will free you from — a bad marriage, an uncomfortable living situation, working for an unappreciative company, etc. You may have to spend some time thinking about it before you start writing, but you'll find the answers flow pretty easily once you stop and look at your situation.

Suggested Resources:

Books:

The Millionaire Next Door, Thomas J. Stanley, Ph.D & William D. Danko, Ph.D. (Pocket Books: Reprint ed., 1998 — ISBN: 0671015206)

Prince Charming Isn't Coming: How Women Get Smart About Money by Barbara Stanny(Penguin USA: 1999 — ISBN: 0140266933)

What's Your Net Worth? Click Your Way To Wealth by Jennifer Openshaw and Sela Ward (Perseus Publishing, March 2002 — ISBN 0738206865) Jennifer Openshaw is the founder of Women's Financial Network. This book provides women with all the advice and access they need to achieve financial security. www.jenifero.com

FIVE-MINUTE EXERCISE #8

What money messages did I receive as a child? _____

_____

_____

_____

_____

Were they positive, abundant messages or negative, lacking messages? _____

_____

_____

_____

_____

_____

Do these messages serve me today as I move toward my goals? _____

_____
_____
_____
_____
_____
_____
_____
_____

How have they affected my ability to achieve financial success/freedom? ___

_____
_____
_____
_____
_____
_____
_____
_____
_____
_____
_____

To me, money means . . .
- Freedom from _____
- Power to _____
- Security to _____
- Safety from _____
- Independence from _____
- Love for _____
- Status in _____
- Happiness because _____
- Material things like _____
- To me, money also means _____

_____
_____

🞭 CHAPTER THIRTEEN 🞭

Abundance in Money and More

> *"The greater part of our happiness or misery depends on our dispositions and not on our circumstances."*
> *–Martha Washington*

HAPPINESS IS NOT FOR SALE

In the last exercise, did you check off happiness as one of the things you think money will buy in your life? That was a trick. Many women who are struggling to find funds to take care of kids, pay rent, go to school, buy clothes and food, and pay the bills every month are miserable. They're unhappy with their lives and firmly believe the answer to all their problems is to win the lottery or marry a millionaire or have Aunt Tillie die and leave them that magic cure-all — Money!

If you've fallen into that trap, let me suggest you look at the tabloids the next time you're standing in line at the grocery store. Each issue features several wealthy people who are anything but happy. Every day newspaper headlines blare the problems of people who have more money than most of us will see in a dozen lifetimes.

So if you want to make money in order to be happy, you might as well put this book down right now. You'll never get there. You might make the money, but the happiness will elude you.

I'm not a psychologist. I am just a woman who's been through a lot and who's taught and mentored hundreds of people. I'm basing what I tell you on personal experience and observation. Every day I hear the stories of people just like you and me. I've learned some lessons are universal.

One of those lessons is that money can't buy happiness. Happiness is internal and comes from deep down inside you. You can't pick it up or bottle it — if you could, you'd already be a zillionaire. There's not a happiness pill you can swallow at breakfast. You can't go into a store and buy a pound of happiness to get you through the week. You can't have a slice of happiness for dessert.

Instead, happiness reflects your attitude, how you look at your world. We've all known people who had nothing, but you could hear them singing while they do their work, smiling brightly at everyone they meet. They're optimistic. They think the future will be better and if it isn't, at least they're happy to be alive and be around the people they love. They have the attitude of gratitude, grateful for whatever they have. They've figured out, in any situation, that the glass looks better if you think it's half full rather than half empty.

In 1979, I visited the Philippines for the first time. This was my parents' homeland but it was my first exposure to a third world country. It was an eye-opener. Ten percent of the people were wealthy and the other 90% lived in poverty. What amazed me was that the poor were some of the happiest people I've ever known. They had no stress. They didn't worry. They simply enjoyed each other's company and celebrated life everyday.

Money, on the other hand, is very much an external. It's like a bandage. It can keep a wound clean and help fight infection, but it's not going to heal you. Healing comes from your immune system and your skin's ability to grow back to together. The bandage simplifies the healing process and makes it more pleasant, just like money can make life more pleasant.

MONEY EQUALS FREEDOM, SECURITY — AND MORE MONEY!

What I hope is that you realize money really means freedom and security. When you are self-sufficient financially, you have the freedom to do whatever you want and the security of knowing you never have to worry about handling any situation. There are going to be problems in your life. Unless you live as protected as a doll under a glass dome, life is going to give you a swift kick from time to time. Stuff happens — and we all have to deal with stuff that is at best unpleasant, and at worst disastrous.

It's also true that life isn't fair. Get over it and move on. There's no sense wasting your time and energy trying to find a paradise where you'll never experience loss or illness or setbacks. If you do find it, you're living on some other planet. But if you have money, you can handle whatever comes along — and you won't have to ask anyone for charity.

MONEY IS A GROWTH AGENT

What money does best is allow you to make more money. We've all heard the expression, "It takes money to make money." That's not necessarily true. You can make money without having money, but once you do have a bank account showing a profit, you can make that money work for you. And you can do it without taking risks. When your money is automatically generating more money for you and automatically depositing it in your bank account each month, then you'll know what freedom and security really means.

Later on we'll discuss ways you can put your money to work, but first, let's examine what you want your new wealth to do for you. Exercise #13 asks you to narrow your goals down to the very specific. What exactly are you going to do with the extra cash you bring in? What will you pay for, ranked by importance? I've given you several different amounts of money. First, pick the one you're most comfortable with. It will probably be the smallest. What would you do if you had that extra money coming in every month without you doing anything unusual? Then, branch out. Let your imagination soar. Think what each of the higher amounts could do for you.

After you've completed the exercise, remind yourself that it's all possible. The only thing holding you back is you.

Donna, a stay-at-home mom with three small children, tried dozens of ways to make money. Her big goal was to earn an extra $50 a week so she could take the family out to Sunday brunch. To earn the cash, she wallpapered houses, held Tupperware™ parties, and babysat for other people's kids. Finally she joined a direct marketing company.

Now Donna simply asked people if they were opened-minded enough to hear about her new business. She spoke highly of a very successful gentleman who could explain how someone working an extra five hours a week could build an income of $5,000 per month. She knew people wouldn't listen to her if they knew her past income-generating history. In this business, if they liked what they heard after five minutes they could find out more — and if not, they wouldn't have to hear about it again. Through appealing to people's desire to have more, through speaking well of someone who could show them how, and through letting them do all the talking, she built a business. It enabled her to live in her dream home and allowed her husband to retire from a 20-year career in the electronics industry,

Today she can afford to take her family to Sunday brunch in France every week if she wanted to. Donna now talks to other women about how they can build the same sort of business with little education and no experience. With just one person believing in you, your life, too, can completely be transformed.

In the next exercise, think about what more money would mean to you. Everyone daydreams about "if only I had......more to spend." This is your time to visualize what extra cash would do for your life. How much more do you need each month to make your dreams come true? Be generous. This isn't the time to be budget conscious. When you understand how much more you need a month, then you'll have a specific goal to shoot for and a clear picture of how important it is for you to reach it.

Suggested Resources:

Books:

The 9 Steps to Financial Freedom: Practical & Spiritual Steps So You Can Stop Worrying by Suze Orman (Crown Publishers Inc: 1997 — ISBN: 0517707918)

Secrets of Six-Figure Women: Surprising Strategies to Up Your Earnings and Change Your Life by Barbara Stanny. (HarperCollins: 2002 — ISBN: 0060185481)

FIVE-MINUTE EXERCISE #13

If I had an extra $100 a month, I would:

1. _____   4. _____
2. _____   5. _____
3. _____   6. _____

If I had an extra $500 a month, I would:

1. _____   4. _____
2. _____   5. _____
3. _____   6. _____

If I had an extra $1000 a month, I would:

1. _____   4. _____
2. _____   5. _____
3. _____   6. _____

If I had an extra $5,000 a month, I would:

1. _____   4. _____
2. _____   5. _____
3. _____   6. _____

If I had an extra $10,000 a month, I would:

1. _____   4. _____
2. _____   5. _____
3. _____   6. _____

If money were not an issue, I would:

1. _____   4. _____
2. _____   5. _____
3. _____   6. _____

Did you set a goal to help someone else? Karma is getting back what you give tenfold. Start today with a plan to help others, no matter how small it is.

THOUGHT PROVOKER: THE POWER OF DOUBLING

If a genie offered you either a bank account with a balance of $100,000 in cash — or an account with one penny, but that balance would double every day for 30 days, which would you choose? Obvious! You'll grab the cash, right? Wrong! Take the penny and have the account balance double daily. Here's how it will work:

Day 1	.02
Day 2	.04
Day 3	.08
Day 4	.16
Day 5	.32
Day 6	.64
Day 7	1.28
Day 8	2.56
Day 9	5.12
Day 10	10.24
Day 11	20.48
Day 12	40.96
Day 13	81.62
Day 14	163.84
Day 15	327.68
Day 16	655.36
Day 17	1,310.72
Day 18	2,621.44
Day 19	5,242.88
Day 20	10,485.76
Day 21	20,971.52
Day 22	41,943.04
Day 23	83,886.08
Day 24	167,772.16
Day 25	335,544.32
Day 26	671,088.64
Day 27	1,342,177.28
Day 28	2,684,354.56
Day 29	5,368,709.12
Day 30	$ 10,737,418.24

Always remember — great fortunes often start with a small investment!
Invest in Yourself!

CHAPTER FOURTEEN

Start with Business Basics

> *"It is not fair to ask of others
> what you are not willing to do yourself."*
> —*Eleanor Roosevelt*

THE BASIC BUSINESS STRUCTURE

Whether you're starting a company with a five million dollar investment or beginning out of your dining room with a $50 cash outlay, you are running a business. The size really doesn't matter because the basic rules always apply.

In this chapter I want to give you a crash course in the basics of being in business. There are things you have to know and do to be successful — and stay out of jail. You will want to get more information on each of the things we discuss, but this will get you started.

Every business combines labor, equipment and materials so it can sell products or services. It's just that simple. As an independent contractor, someone who works for herself instead of being employed by a company, you can begin your business without incorporating. You will want to check with your local city government to see if you need a business license. These licenses aren't usually expensive but they give you credibility as a commercial enterprise. Every community has different laws. Some require everyone who earns money out of their home to be licensed, including writers and artists. Others are much more lenient and only require a license if you are actually selling a tangible product.

YOUR MISSION STATEMENT

First of all, every business exists to sell something. It doesn't have to be a product like cookies or blankets or widgets. It can be your talent, your services, your knowledge, your experience or your time. This is your purpose for being in business. It's what you do and whether you're preparing taxes, recruiting, catering, writing, selling home-made booties for newborns, showing houses to prospective buyers, or distributing vitamins for a network marketing company, you have a mission to accomplish.

Every company has a mission statement. In fact, in recent years these short definitions of what your purpose is have become so popular that many families and churches have identified their reason for being.

To write a mission statement for your business, think about what it is you want to accomplish with your product or service. The statement should be no longer than a paragraph, the shorter the better. Try and incorporate what it is you're going to bring to other people with your business. For instance, my mission statement for the *Gimme Five!* Method might be:

> My *Gimme Five!* mission is to educate, mentor, teach, guide and assist people to know themselves, identify their dreams, handle their money, work with people and maximize their options in the pursuit and realization of their goals for a better life through books, seminars, speeches, and making myself available to groups across the country.

It doesn't have to be any longer than that. You can see how in 54 words I have summed up the entire scope of the book and what I'm doing to spread the *Gimme Five!* Method message across as wide an audience as possible.

Before going on, spend a few minutes and begin to think about the elements you want to include in your mission statement. I'd suggest you use scrap paper to begin. It often takes several tries until it says exactly what you want. When you're done, write your personal mission statement below.

My Mission Statement

_____

_____

_____

_____

_____

Over time your mission statement may change as your business changes. What's important is that you keep it updated so it is a consistent reflection of what you're doing and a constant reminder of your purpose.

WHAT'S IN A NAME?

Every business has to have a name. Sounds simple enough to name your company, but actually it's anything but. The name has to be memorable, easy to spell and descriptive of what you do. That can be a tall order.

Some people name their businesses after themselves: Sally Smith & Company, Anderson & Associates, Mary Jones Jewelry. If it is your special expertise people will be buying, then it makes sense to have your name in the company name.

You might want to have a name that descriptive of what you do. K.D. Sullivan's proofreading and editing company is called Creative Solutions because that's what she offers. Mighty Maids® is obviously a home cleaning service. Terri Lonier, who is one of the country's best-known entrepreneur advisors, calls her company Working Solo®. I named my company Freedom Seminars because freedom is what I offer the attendees.

Once you come up with a name, go through your local phones books and make sure there isn't another company using it already. You should also go to Google.com or one of the other search engines and type in the name you've chosen to see what comes up.

(If you decide to incorporate down the road you'll have to pay for a search to make sure you aren't treading on anyone's trademarked toes. This is another reason to incorporate your name — less chance of it being duplicated.)

THE NUTS AND BOLTS

When the name and mission statement are in place, you will want to have business cards and letterhead. At first, you can fake letterhead on the computer but business cards are a necessity. There are companies on the Internet that will send you 100 free cards to showcase their services. Kinko's and other printers will make cards for you. They are an inexpensive way to advertise and market your new product or service.

Keep the design simple on a standard size single card with lettering large enough to be read easily. Include your name, your company name, a line about the product or service you provide, your address, phone, fax, and email. If you use your cell phone routinely, include that. Also list your website if you have one.

Another essential for a new business is a dedicated space. It doesn't have to be large. A card table in the corner of the bedroom can work for starters, but ideally you will have a room you can set aside. This is where your computer, a small file case, desk, chair and telephone will live. It's wise to get a dedicated line for your business telephone so you can deduct the cost from your taxes without giving your CPA indigestion.

Make the space as attractive as possible. You'll be spending a lot of time there for a while. Lisa Kanarak has great materials on how to organize your home office. (See the resources listed at the end of this chapter.)

LAWS AND TAXES

Since I just mentioned your CPA, let's talk a minute about the professional help you're going to need. When you're working for yourself, you're responsible for paying your own taxes. The people who hire you or to whom you sell something aren't responsible for deducting social security and income tax from what they pay you. You will now pay the U.S. government — and your state and city taxes where applicable -four times a year.

Unless you're handy with numbers, you will want someone to do the figuring for you. Ask other people in your situation for a recommendation to a trustworthy Certified Public Accountant who can prepare your forms for you. If you use a standard computer program like QuickBooks®, you can do most things by email and probably never have to spend time in your CPA's office. (One friend's CPA is in Phoenix. She lives in Chicago. They haven't seen each other in years and it works just fine.)

While you may not need a lawyer often, situations will arise in which you want to someone with a legal eye to read a contract, or have a letter sent on a lawyer's stationery, or talk about your options in a specific situation. Again, ask your friends for recommendations or check with the local Bar Association.

The Five-Minute Quiz:

No matter what size business you are going into, you should go through the exercise of making a business plan. Your business plan gives overall direction to your company. In addition to clearly stating your main purpose for being in business and outlining your competitive advantage, it communicates the same focus to you, to anyone working with you, and to your investors. Putting together a business plan requires you first to think of the big picture, and then to sweat out the nitty-gritty details.

Name of Business: _____

Product or Service offered: _____

_____

_____

Who are your customers: _____

_____

Where are they, how are you going to reach them: _____

_____

Who is your competition: _____

_____

What is your competitive advantage?: _____

_____

Nine out of ten businesses fail in the first year because of inadequate capital and cash flow management. What costs are involved to start your business and to provide your services, produce your product, market and support your customers on an on-going basis: _____

_____

_____

_____

You'll also be setting goals and checkpoints that you can use to evaluate your progress in the months ahead so you can be certain you're moving in the right direction.

How much money do you need to start: _____

What is the source of initial money to start: _____

_____

_____

Where is your business located:_____

What is the legal form (sole proprietorship, partnership or corporation): __

_____

What sales do you need to break even: _____

What are your first year sales goals: _____

What are your first year profit goals: _____

_____

Even if you never ask an investor for a dime, even if you never hire anyone else to work the business with you, it's still an essential exercise. You want to know where you're going and how you're going to get there. When we talk about accountability in Chapter 23, you'll find your business plan can keep you on track and moving forward in the right direction.

There are as many types of business plans as there are businesses. A business plan can be four or five pages or ten times that size. It depends on what your situation requires.

For basic information, check the Small Business Administration. They have offices in most cities and an extensive website (www.sba.gov) that will give you detailed information on how to write a plan that will work for you. There is also an organization called SCORE that is comprised of retired executives who can assist, guide and mentor you through this business process. (www.score.org)

The Business Plans Kit for Dummies book in the resources box at the end of this chapter includes a CD-ROM that will provide the template so you have only to fill in the blanks. You'll find several simple guides in any bookstore or library.

GETTING IT ALL TOGETHER

This chapter isn't meant to replace a course in business. It's just a few tips you need to know before you go off into the heady world of making money. In the exercise, list and prioritize what you need to do before putting out your shingle and opening your door to customers. I've put some items in for you and left lots of space for you to add on to the list. When you've accomplished a task, check it off. Nothing looks better than a page of tasks that have been checked off completed.

Suggested Resources:

Books:

Working Solo: The Real Guide to Freedom & Financial Success with Your Own Business, 2nd Edition , by Terri Lonier(John Wiley & Sons:1998 — ISBN: 0471247138)

Organizing Your Home Business by Lisa Kanarek(Made Ez Products:2002 — ISBN: 1563825155

Business Plans Kit for Dummies (With CD-ROM) by Steven D. Peterson and Peter E. Jaret (For Dummies; Book and CD-ROM: 2001- ISBN: 0764553658)

10 Commandments of Small-Business Success by Marguerite Kirk(Bookhome Publishers:1999 — ISBN:1889438251)

Software:

QuickBooks, Quicken Financial Services: www.quickbooks.com

Websites:

Small Business Association — www.sba.gov
This site is chock-full of information that will be useful to you when starting up.

www.workingsolo.com (lots of information from Terri Lonier on running a one-person business.)

www.jian.com (provides a variety of business tools ranging from comprehensive business plans to contract templates)

www.homelifeoffice.com (Lisa Kanarek gives tons of tips on how to find the space for your home office and organize it for optimum productivity.)

Exercise #14

Before I open my door and begin my business, I have to make sure the following tasks have been completed:

Done/Task

____ Decided on what my new business will be
____ Wrote my Mission Statement
____ Decided on a business name
____ Checked to see name is not already taken
____ Identified and contacted a financial advisor (CPA)
____ Identified and contacted a legal advisor
____ Checked need for a business license
____ Ordered business cards, letterhead
____ Identified space to use as an office
____ Had business phone installed
____ Purchased basic supplies
____ Wrote my business plan
____ Spread the word to friends, associates, and family that I am in business

As a business person, you'll find you are always making lists. Keep writing down new things that have to be accomplished and checking them off. Some days those check marks are your best reward.

_____
_____
_____
_____
_____
_____
_____
_____
_____
_____

Make Money, Save Money, Grow Your Money

> *"A woman must have money and a room of her own."*
> *—Virginia Woolf*

WOMEN AND MONEY

It was interesting to try and find a quotation about money from a woman to start this chapter. I have about a dozen books of quotations by women and several dozen general quotation books. In the general quotation anthologies, men said a lot about money, but the subject was barely touched on in the women's collections. Why? I think it's because women have been taught from the earliest time of our civilization that money is a man's business and women who talked about it were somehow tainted.

Let's dispel that myth right now. Women need to understand how money works, how to use it, grow it, spend it and save it. Pure and simple, women have to catch up with men in the financial arena.

Unfortunately, as a society we don't train our young people of either gender about managing money. In June, 2003, *The New York Times* reported some high schools are beginning to offer classes in balancing checkbooks, paying bills and living on a budget for their seniors heading off to college. There are also several websites, sponsored by organizations like Junior Achievement (www.japersonal-finance.com), the Securities Industry Foundation for Economic Education (www.smgww.org), and Visa (www.practicalmoney-skills.com) as well as government sites (www.-

treas.gov/kids) that explain the work of the United States Mint and the Bureau of Public Debt among others.

These and other sites aimed at elementary through high school grades can also be rich learning grounds for adults who want to brush up on the basics in an entertaining way.

Don't Blow It, Grow It

I mentioned earlier that most lottery winners don't have any money left within 24 months. It is a huge temptation when money becomes available to "spend it just this once." That's a lot like saying "I'll only have one bite of chocolate cake" when you're on a diet. All those "just this once" occasions build up and before you know it, you're right back where you were before.

I'm not a money professional, but I've given you some books and other tools at the end of this chapter which you can use to help you choose the most intelligent ways to ensure your money makes money for you. You should also look into adult finance courses at your local community college or work with a licensed financial advisor who can help you invest wisely.

Side-Step the Con Artists

One important rule to remember — if any deal sounds too good to be true, it almost undoubtedly is! Get rich schemes only work for the person offering them, not for the hopeful who take the bait.

Con artists know "there's a sucker born every minute" and that the more desperate we are for money, the less cautious we are about what we'll do to get it. This explains the email scams that continue to pop up on our computer screens in which supposed millionaires in third world countries desperately need our help. These con artists pose as the representative of a prince or widow of some high-ranking official in a country like Nigeria. The person needs to move millions of dollars out of their country but obviously can't do it under their own name. All the sucker needs to do is send their bank account number and other classified financial information. The money will be wired to the sucker's account and as a thank you, the sucker will be gifted with an unbelievably large share of the money.

Sounds ridiculous, doesn't it? How could millions of dollars suddenly run through your bank account without the U.S. government showing up on your doorstep within a matter of hours? If it weren't illegal, why would the scammers need you? Why not go directly to an American bank? When you start asking logical questions, the whole house of cards falls apart. In fact, all the sucker is doing is handing over complete financial access to a crook.

Here's the frightening part: If people weren't falling for the racket, the emails would end right now. Instead, it's not uncommon for any email address to get several solicitations a week. If it weren't working, the crooks would be on to another scam.

Of course, the people who are burned most badly are the people least able to afford it, so be careful!

THE MAGIC WORDS: BUDGET AND SAVE

My first two pieces of advice for the beginner are to make a budget you can stick to, and save at least 10% of everything you earn. Sure, it means you're not going to have as much money available for spending today, but you will have a cushion to fall back on and there's great comfort in that. According to *Good Housekeeping* magazine, women enjoy shopping and shop for fun. Compared to men, we are twice as likely to buy things we just don't need.

Exercise #15 is a budget form for you to work with. You can adapt it to fit your life and needs — and it will undoubtedly take you more than five minutes — but it is one of the most important exercises you'll ever complete.

Dina is 60 and single, plans to retire in two years, and is in excellent financial health. Working in a support capacity for an insurance company, she has never made a great deal of money but she has definite plans for where every penny will be spent.

She has cleared her mortgage, keeps to a strict budget, and has always saved 30% of her salary. That means she has often had less than $30,000 a year of disposable income.

She drives a nice car but doesn't spend cash on extras like cable or high-speed computer connections. She is always looking for ways to save a few pennies on water and other utilities. She uses a cell phone for long distance on the lowest cost plan available and has minimal service on her home phone. She's a member of a low-risk investment club and keeps a close watch on her company sponsored 401K stock value. Right next to her favorite chair you'll find a calculator sitting on top of her checkbook. She knows where every penny of her money is spent.

Dina may not spend a lot of time shopping or going on expensive vacations or buying useless things on impulse, but she lives in a beautiful house, has everything she needs, and best of all, can retire knowing that she can live comfortably the rest of her life…and she did it on a very modest income.

It's so easy to spend money, especially money you don't have (credit cards). Personally, I don't do all the things Dina does, but I do a lot of them. I certainly keep to a budget, which isn't easy with a husband and two young children providing me with constant opportunities to spend. But I've been flat broke. I know what it feels like to not have enough money to buy food, let alone pay the rent, and I don't ever plan to be in that situation again. What's more, no matter what my husband earns, I know better than to depend on anyone else but myself for my own security. That's the only way I can sleep soundly at night.

Five Steps to Financial Bliss

Here are some of the proven ways that will help you save money and then make that money work for you.

1. Determine your budget to meet financial goals (income, house, education, vacation, hobbies, retirement, perhaps care for elderly parents, etc.)
2. Work toward paying off all outstanding balances on your credit cards and then pay all new charges at the end of each month to avoid high finance charges. Seek financial help if necessary. Consumer credit counselors will contact creditors, reduce interest rates and restructure payments at no charge. Get a copy of your credit report now.
3. First — pay yourself:
   • 10% for emergencies (build up a three- to six-month reserve);
   • 10% for investments (take advantage of tax-deferred and pre-tax programs offered by your employer);

   According the Security and Exchange Commission report, "The Facts on Savings and Investing," two-thirds of American

households will fail to realize one or more life goals because they lack a comprehensive financial plan.
• 10% percent tithed to a church or charity. No matter how tough things are, there's always someone in worse trouble. Giving to help another without expectation of return is its own reward.

Many people believe in Karma — whatever you give, you will get back tenfold.

A few years ago, I did my due diligence looking for a kid's play structure. At Costco, I bought one for $1,000 that sold for $2,500 at the local kids specialty play structure store. We sold our house to a couple that had no children and no use for the play structure my kids had now outgrown.

My in-laws live next to a family with six children who couldn't afford a play structure, so we gave them ours. When we moved to our new house, the gardener knew of someone who wanted to give away their more advanced play structure for older children. They gave it to us for free as long as we paid to have it moved. They originally paid over $10,000 for it at an auction!

It's just a little personal proof that as you give, so shall you receive tenfold. The Universal Law of giving has shown us many times that giving precedes success. Just ask people who are successful, people who are positive and generous, they will often tell you that before they were successful, they were givers even if it was difficult for them financially. Others are generous with their time or knowledge, giving what they can.

4. Educate yourself on your options:
    • Find ways to generate additional income through learning new skills or taking classes so you can get a better job, find employment as an independent contractor, or to start or buy a business;
    • Keep your mind and ears open to opportunities to generate residual income.
    • Set up a dummy trading account in a notebook and trade stocks on paper before you ever put a penny of your own into the market.

    (You'll find more info when you get to the Smart Options section of this book.)

5. Discipline yourself daily with your choices.
    - $2.50 latte five days a week for two months = $100.00
    - If you take just $100 and add $100 every year and invest it at 11% over 10 years at = $1,700, 20 years = $6,500, 30 years = $20,120, 40 years = $58,829 and 50 years = $168,706.

    Instead, save the latte money and reward yourself periodically. A $20 pedicure, $40 dinner and movie or $60 massage will do you a lot more good than a paper cup of coffee and milk you can make at home for pennies.

WAYS TO SAVE DOLLARS THAT MAKE SENSE

Let me give you a few methods to save money. No one of these is going to save you a fortune, but when done together, you'll be amazed at how much you can painlessly put aside each year.

$- **Use coupons.** I have one friend who cuts out coupons and puts them in her handbag, but invariably forgets to use them at the store. All that random looking and clipping just wastes the money her time is worth. Instead, make out a grocery list and paper clip the relevant coupons to the list. That way you'll have them with you at the checkout counter. Remember, your time is worth money so don't spend all your valuable hours looking for, cutting out and organizing coupons. This is what's called being "penny-wise and pound-foolish."

Now, *here's the secret.* Look at how much money you saved — most grocery stores put that number on the receipt — and as soon as you get home take that amount of cash and put it in your savings account. Otherwise, you didn't save money; you just gave yourself more money to spend.

$- **Save your change.** Designate a receptacle and a place in your home — Ellen uses a big glass ornamental jar she got at a budget import store, Patty uses a five gallon water jar, and both keep them on the floor next to the hall table right inside the front door — and every time they come home they empty their change purses into that receptacles. You can increase the amount of change you receive if you always pay with paper money. Even if the total due is $3.05, you have every right to expect the merchant to give you

95¢ in coins. It's amazingly easy for you to save $25 or more a month this way. When the jar gets full, take the coins to the bank and deposit them in your savings account.

$- **Sell your discards.** Whether you organize a garage sale, rent a table at a flea market, or sell your stuff on the Internet, there is good money waiting to be made. The secret -- if you don't absolutely need the money to live on, put it in savings. It's available to you for necessities but just difficult enough to access that you won't be tempted to use it to splurge on impulse purchases.

$- **Shop with a list at supermarkets.** There's a reason why the milk is at the back of the store, 60% of supermarket purchases are NOT planned! Make your list and stick to it. Shop on line if possible to prevent you from picking up those impulse purchases or sale items. This will save you time and money.

$- **Buy items from consignment centers, discount stores and thrift shops.**

While looking for a new dining room set at "fine furniture stores," I stopped in a consignment store in an upscale neighborhood. There I found a very close match to the $8,000 set I wanted — the price tag read $2,000. The set had been in a model home and had never been used.

You can also get wonderful buys on clothes in resale shops. One young woman in San Francisco bought all her clothes from thrift shops for several years after college. Her job necessitated that she look great every day on a less than lavish salary. She found super bargains — many with the price tags still attached. Now that she can afford more traditional stores, she misses the excitement of finding the perfect outfit for a tenth the price.

Brand names at bargain prices will satisfy your desire to look good and keep you on track financially. One friend showed me the leather coat she bought for $450 at a "fine" retail store. I didn't have the heart to tell her I had purchased the identical coat for $150 from a discount retail outlet.

$- **End of season purchases.** Also, pay attention to WHEN you are buying. There is always a cycle of moving out seasonal items and clothing at which time you can purchase take advantage of even deeper discounts. If you've just got to have something new, you get an incredible bargain with end-of-season items discounted up to 75% or more. The best time to pick up gifts are after Christmas. For those occasional birthday or thank you gifts you just can't beat the price. And for the most amazing savings of all, make your end-of-season purchases at discount stores!

$- **Estate sales and garage sales.** One of the ladies I worked with loved going to garage sales and picking up old record albums. People would sell these literally for a song. To the right person, many of them were highly prized collectibles that she sells through the newspaper or on the Internet. If you have a particular hobby or passion for specific items, you'll be amazed of what others are selling for pocket change. You can find cookbooks, artwork, office supplies and garden tools and so much more for 10¢ on the dollar.

Simple Financial Ideas

There's no way I can distill a complete financial plan into a few pages and I'm not even going to try. If you need this book to increase your income and become self-sufficient financially, you probably won't have to worry about complicated financial structures for a few months. When that time comes, you'll want to make sure you have enough insurance, your will is up-to-date and you have a trust in place. Until then, this is basic information that can help you get started.

The bookstore shelves are loaded with books on how to manage money. I have listed some of my favorites below. You can't go wrong with the "Dummies" books or "Idiots Guides," both of which feature sensible, easy-to-understand information from reputable sources on a wide range of basic topics. They have excellent financial titles.

If you're comfortable on the Internet, there are a number of very useful websites that can walk you through the basics of money management. A particularly useful free site is the American Savings Education Council (ASEC). At www.asec.org you'll find all sorts of information on budgets, savings, and growing money at all stages of your life. Their "Ballpark E$timate" form, which shows you how to plan for retirement starting today, is recommended on a number of other sites, from government to private financial companies. Since it's free, there's no excuse for not getting it now.

Don't Wait, Start NOW!

There's an old English proverb that says, "One of these days is none of these days." If you don't set a date — preferably today's! — as the start date for working toward your goal, you'll never get there. While Scarlett O'Hara thought tomorrow would be soon enough, you and I know it's too far in the future. The most important thing is that you start doing something right now to earn, preserve and grow your money.

Giving an Unselfish Gift Rewards Immensely – It's Simply Priceless

Talk to successful people and you'll find those that are happy are grateful for what they have and appreciate the people around them and find tremendous joy in helping others. I'm grateful for my parents who instilled in me a strong work ethic and respect for others. There was never a lot of money but there was always an opportunity to give and volunteer to help others. I've come to know that money can be powerful in helping others. Think of what you can do to help someone else.

My friend Dora lost her job as an engineer. She started her own company and built an incredible international sales team. She bought her mother a house and cares for her every need. She also built a home for the homeless in Atlanta where families could learn new skills and find employment knowing their children would be cared for.

* * * * * * * * *

Trish Millines Dziko became a wealthy women after eight years with Microsoft. She quit her job and launched a non-profit foundation that gives technical training to minority youngsters. She has trained over 500 young people and all but one of the 74 interns who have graduated from the teen program have gone on to college. As far as she's concerned, the "Good Life" is one she's already living.

* * * * * * * * *

Diane Cornman-Levy, a top notch teacher, desired to make an even bigger difference. In 1998 she created Journey Home, a nonprofit organization that offers job training, counseling and support services to the home-less. "Helping people in distress to realize their full potential. You can't put a price on that."

SUCCESS TECHNIQUE #3

Set an appointment with yourself each month and review your financial standing. Rate your success at earning, savings and ability to achieve your monthly goal.

Suggested Resources:

Books:

Secrets of Six-Figure Women: Surprising Strategies to Up Your Earnings and Change Your Life by Barbara Stanny. (HarperCollins: 2002 — ISBN: 0060185481)

Smart Women Finish Rich by David Bach (Broadway Books: 1999 — ISBN: 0767902424))

Get Clark Smart: The Ultimate Guide to Getting Rich from America's Money-Saving Expert by Howard Clark and Mark Meltzer (Hyperion Press: 2002 — ISBN: 078688777X)

The Richest Man in Babylon by George S. Clason (Signet: ISBN: 0-451-16520-9) "Babylonian parables," hailed as the greatest of all inspirational works on the subject of thrift, financial planning and personal wealth.

Websites:

www.wfn.com — Women's Financial Network, learn about investing, planning and financial information, budgeting tools and paper trading tools online.

www.jennifero.com — Author of What's Your Net Worth, click your way to weath. Provides financial tools, tips and information to reach your financial goals

Free Online Budget Help: www.mvelopes.com

"Ballpark E$timate Worksheet" American Savings Education Council — www.asec.org (ASEC, Suite 600, 2121 K Street NW, Washington, DC 20037-1896)

INSTRUCTIONS FOR EXERCISE #15A

Commitment: Doing what you said you would do, long after the mood you said it in has passed. Make a commitment to yourself, your family and your financial well being by filling out the promise below.

I, _____, promise to review my financial well-being every month, by reviewing my current financial standing and evaluating financial decision I have made for the month and adjusting them accordingly.

I will also have quarterly meetings with (myself, my spouse, my kids) to insure we all agree to make decisions to move us towards our goals.

I will also have yearly financial check-up to determine if there are any major adjustment to my monthly plan to achieve my financial goals.

_____   _____
Signed   Date

INSTRUCTIONS FOR EXERCISE #15B

Often people are afraid of looking at this exercise and hesitate — or even refuse — to complete it. The facts you fill in often come as a rude awakening. In your gut you know you're out of control and you just don't want to face it. Don't kid yourself. What if something were to happen to you, if you were unable to work due to an accident? What would happen to your family, quality of life and sanity?

Most people plan their vacations better than their lives. To have a great vacation, you must know where you are, where you are going, how you're going to get there, how much it's going to cost, and when you'll return. This exercise asks much the same questions and is essential to your health, happiness and financial stability. No excuses. Just do it now.

What's your net worth? Your balance sheet is a snapshot of where you stand financially today.

Fill out the numbers in the following exercise sheet. In the first column, write down how much you spend for each category. In the second column, how much you can trim to meet your financial goals. In an ideal world, the total on the actual costs will be less than your monthly budget figure above. Otherwise, you need to trim costs until they are in line. In the third column, you'll have your new budgeted allowance for each category and you can start crawling, walking, then running down the path to financial freedom. Be sure to evaluate how you are doing each month. Make a date with yourself and keep your commitment. You can do it!

ASSETS	current	one-year goal	five-year goal
Cash on hand	_____	_____	_____
Bank account(s)	_____	_____	_____
Brokerage acct.(s)	_____	_____	_____
Car	_____	_____	_____
House	_____	_____	_____
Furnishings	_____	_____	_____
Retirement Plan(s)	_____	_____	_____
TOTAL ASSETS	_____	_____	_____

LIABILITIES	current	one-year goal	five-year goal
Credit card debt	_____	_____	_____
Installment debt	_____	_____	_____
(furniture, car loans, student loans etc.)			
House	_____	_____	_____

TOTAL LIABILITIES	_____	_____	_____
NET WORTH	_____	_____	_____
(Assets - Liabilities)			

Now you've got to look at your Income Statement. How much do you have coming in and going out each month? Determine what your budget needs to be to help you meet your financial goal. _____

_____

_____

_____

Calculate how much money you make each year. This figure should include all the income you receive from any source, including social security, disability, interest, etc. $_____

Deduct all taxes and payroll deductions.$ _____

Divide this figure by 12 to get your monthly budget figure.$ _____

EXERCISE # 15C

_____'s **Budget**

Fixed Expenses	Actual Cost	Trim Costs	New Costs
Mortgage/rent			
Savings			
Gas/Electric/Oil			
Phone(s)			
Water			
Garbage			
Insurance			
Credit card payments			
Loan repayments			
Car payments			
School/college expenses			
Membership dues			
Food			
Household help/babysitting			
Cable/Dish T-			
Variable Expenses			
Clothing			
Doctor/Dentist			
Pharmacy			
Entertainment			
Eating out			
Books/magazines			
Home repairs			
Car repairs			
Gasoline			
Cleaning/personal care			
Church/charities			
Furniture/appliances			
Gifts			
Hobbies			
Vacation			
TOTALS			

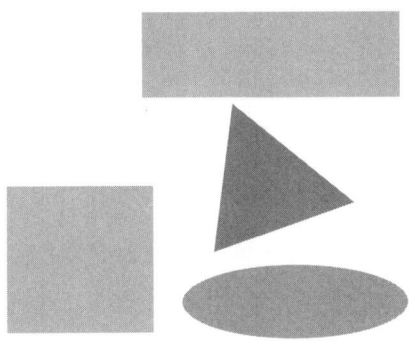

Section IV:
Become People-Smart

GIMME FIVE! RULE NUMBER FOUR

**"The more you understand people,
the more successful you will be."**

❦ CHAPTER SIXTEEN ❧

The Power of a Championship Circle

> " I think we're here for each other. "
> —Carol Burnett

BUILD YOUR OWN FIREWALL

Long before it was adapted by the computer industry, "firewall" referred to an impenetrable barrier that prevented fire from spreading. Anything deemed truly valuable should be protected behind a firewall and in the case of human endeavor, that means being circled by friends and experts. I call it the Championship Circle.

In his book, *Think and Grow Rich,* Napoleon Hill recounts that during World War I, a Chicago newspaper's editorial dubbed Henry Ford "an ignorant pacifist." The automotive pioneer sued the newspaper for libel and when the case came to trial, defense attorneys tried to prove Ford's ignorance to the jury. The lawyers asked him questions about history and literature to test his general knowledge. Finally, Ford had had enough. He said: "I have a row of electric push-buttons on my desk and by pushing the right button I can summon to my aid men who can answer any question I desire to ask concerning the business to which I am devoting most of my efforts…why should I clutter up my mind with general knowledge…when I have men around me who can supply any knowledge I require?" He won the case.

What Henry Ford had to rely on was a Championship Circle. In other words, he had built a firewall of knowledgeable people he could turn to for help. Most people who are new to business are overwhelmed by the amount of information they need and don't have. Don't worry about what you don't know. You can always find the information. Albert Einstein said it was silly to memorize anything you could look up — and that was before the Internet put experts at our fingertips in a mouse click. Add a Championship Circle to the other information resources — along with mentors and the Master Mind group we will talk about in Chapter 20 — and you have an unbeatable fund of knowledge from which you can draw.

We all need access to experts who can answer our questions and fill in our blanks. That's why there is nothing more critical to success than building a team — your Championship Circle — people who surround you, help you, work with you, encourage you, and keep you moving forward in the right direction.

CHOOSING YOUR CHAMPIONSHIP CIRCLE

Who are the people you want on your team, in your Championship Circle? That's for you to decide. I suggest you select people who will complement your skill set and knowledge, people who are success-oriented and driven, not a "yes" team who will just tell you what you want to hear.

But I'd like you to remember a few facts. First, we usually hang out with our peers. The people we spend time with are very likely much like us…about the same income, the same educational background, the same life experiences. Why? Because they make us feel comfortable. Like an old chair, we know their every curve and contour. We don't have to sit up straight or protect the new upholstery. That may be fine with chairs, but with friends it means we're not spending enough time around people who will help us grow.

Studies show that usually our income is the average of the incomes of the five people we spend the most time with. If your income is on the low end of the scale, these aren't the friends who'll be urging you to move into a higher tax bracket. You're their "old chair" and your success is guaranteed to make them uncomfortable. Who would want that?

Now don't think you can't have friends with whom you enjoy going to the movies or sharing an evening or game of cards. Of course you can. But they probably aren't going to be the people in your _Gimme Five!_ Champion Circle. Those people are going to be the pushers and pullers who make you work hard to be better than you have ever been.

If you've participated seriously in a sport you understand this concept. You get better by "playing up," playing with someone better than you. It's the same in life. If you're changing direction not only will you need new skills, you'll need new knowledge and contacts. You have to expand your circle of influence. Six degrees of separation will get you to the people who know what you need to know or who have the contacts to get you to where you need to be.

The concept of six degrees of separation is that you are six people removed from anyone in the world. Bringing this down to a more practical example, you want to talk to G but it seems impossible. However, you meet A whose brother B works with C whose college roommate E lives next door to F whose aunt's best friend is G. That's how it works. The secret it to nudge the world to look for the people you want to know. You'll find a way to get to them through creative networking. I do it all the time.

PICKING PEOPLE IS LIKE SORTING APPLES

I try and divide people into three groups, a little like sorting apples. There are many varieties of apples but let's say you go to the grocery store and want a red delicious apple, not a green granny smith apple or a golden delicious apple but a red delicious apple. If you're at the grocery store looking at the red delicious variety of apples and see red apples, green apples and rotten apples sitting in the bin, you know you're going to put the red apple in your bag. Red ripe apples are ready to eat, juicy and delicious. Green apples won't be ready to eat for several days and never taste as good as those that ripened on the tree. Of course, rotten apples are bruised, mushy and runny, and you definitely don't put them in your bag. Deciding whom to spend time with is much the same process.

Red apples are people who are successful, positive people who are full of information and knowledge. When you're around them you feel good (perhaps even intimidated). These are the ripe apple people you want to spend 80% of your time with or looking for.

Green apples are people who don't share your mindset and may not be as progressive or active in the pursuit of their goals, but you enjoy their company. You don't have time to wait for them to mature enough to be enjoyed, so spend no more than 20% of your time with them.

Rotten apples are unhappy, excuse-filled, critical and negative. Stay as far away from them as you can.

Who Belongs in Your Championship Circle?

I've spent a fair amount of space warning you about people who will bring you down and destroy your dream. Now it's time to think about those who you can count on to be on your team, to cheer you on, and to help you as you take this journey to a new life. These are the people who are delighted when you have good news and stand beside you when the news isn't as positive. They truly wish you the very best and will go out of their way to help you achieve it. They have skills you don't have but are happy to instruct you.

If you have one person in your life who meets that description, you are truly blessed. You probably have more than one who meets a good part of it. This is the time you want to talk to them and tell them what you're planning and how you're going to go about it. In a perfect world, you may have a friend who will join you in the work you're going to be doing. It might be a neighbor who'll walk with you every morning or a roommate who'll empty the sugar and fat out of your cupboards to help you stick to a diet.

If you're married, your spouse may give you strength and lead the cheers when you succeed. If they're old enough, perhaps your children will rally around to help you. In network marketing companies, your sponsor will be your coach and the other members of the team will cheer every small victory.

Don't think for a minute we don't need this kind of encouragement. Recent studies have shown that of all the weight loss groups, Weight Watchers™ has the most success. They are also the group that most actively gives visible and verbal rewards for even the smallest weight loss, without ever laying blame on the weeks when the program didn't work.

Even the most solitary person wants to hear applause and if you're going to make really big money, you need a lot of it because you need a lot of people to help you.

Since my divorce, I don't have any friends and with my schedule I don't have time to make any.

I'm too shy to go up to people I don't know. I'd rather stay by myself.

The parents at my kids' school are much younger than I am. They think I'm from another generation.

The people I work with don't have anything in common with me.

I'm new in the city and everyone's unfriendly here.

These are just some of the excuses I've heard. I don't buy any of them. When my parents came to California from the Philippines, they didn't know anyone and they didn't speak English very well. They found friends but they had to work at it — and so do you.

Keep in mind that if you want to have a friend, you have to be a friend. Friendship is a reciprocal activity. You'll be expected to cheer on your friends just as they are rooting for you.

Develop Your Champion Circle Exercises

If you kept the Time Diary as I suggested, you have isolated five hours each week that you can devote to meeting your goals. One of those goals has to be making friends. It's one of those little steps we talked about.

There are two exercises in this chapter. The first one asks you to do something very basic and fundamental to opening up your world of contacts which will equal success in life and business. Write down the names of everyone you know. You may have it in a database on your computer. In that case, you can just print it out.

Every person you know, however casually, is a potential customer, client or part of your cheering section. Once you've gathered all the names, check off the "A" List: The Ripe Apples, those people you think would be the most open to hearing from you. Don't skip this step because these people are your most important resource. It can make the difference between soaring success and dragging difficulty.

You should know that the people who have the information you need are most likely people you don't know at this moment. You'll find these people when you contact your immediate circle of family, friends and acquaintances — and when you use the FORMula (coming up) to attain the contacts and knowledge to pursuit your goal. The best part is these people don't know you and won't prejudge you on your past history.

In Exercise #16B, I've given you six lines on which you can identify the friends you can count on to help and encourage you. If you can put a name on every line, you are a very lucky person.

For those of you who need to find new friends, I've put together a list of possible places where you can meet people who have common interests. If you take an evening class at a community college, you'll find people who have curiosity about the same subject. At any of your child's functions you'll meet parents you can interact with. Hobby stores offer classes where you'll find others who are also perfecting their skills.

One warning. I've included the Internet because a lot of people have found rewarding friendships and associations online, but I caution you to be very wary about the people you're writing to until you're certain they are who they say they are. Never give out your home address. If you meet, do it in a neutral setting like a restaurant or the mall. Make certain people are around. If the person you're becoming friendly with is for real, they'll be just as cautious about you.

See how many places you can check off as possible sources of new friends. Then don't just sit there ... go do something!

Suggested Resources:

Books:

Teamwork Makes the Dreamwork by John C. Maxwell. (J Countryman Books: 2002 — ISBN: 0849955084)

Write It Down Make It Happen: Knowing What You Want And Getting It by Henriette Klauser. (Simon & Schuster:2001 — ISBN: 0684850028)

EXERCISE #16A: WHO DO YOU KNOW?

Before you start the exercise, think about this. If I gave you a bucket of 100 oysters and told you there were five pearls in the bucket, each worth $10,000, would you:

a)   Open the first five, find no oysters and convince yourself there aren't any, decide it's too much work and give up?

b)   Go through the first 50, find two and decide you're satisfied and stop there.

c)   Go through all 100 to find all five?

> Here's the secret — someone you know in turn knows someone else who will lead you to the person you have to reach if you're going to get the information, resource or contact who can help you accomplish your goal. Just think: Every person you know also knows 100+ people!!! You have just expanded your world tenfold!

On the following page, make a list of everyone you know — everyone! You should have a minimum of 100 names (oysters).

Look at your list and put a (*) if this is someone you respect, look up to and admire. Put a(+) if this is a peer (someone with the same education, social economic background, and income). Put a(—) if this is someone who looks up to you.

Pick the top 25 people marked with (*) or (+) who you can contact in the next five days to be part of your new endeavor. Contact five people a day for the next five days using your listening skills and the FORMula to build bridges and gain the information or contacts you'll need to find your mentor and start building your Champion Circle team.

	Name/occupation	Phone Number	*/+	Call Date	Comment
1.					
2.					
3.					
4.					
5.					
6.					
7.					
8.					
9.					
10					
11					
12					
13					
14					
15					
16					
17					
18					
19					
20					
21					
22					
23					
24					
25					
26					
27					
28					
29					
30					
31					
32					
33					
34					
35					

	Name/occupation	Phone Number	*/+	Call Date	Comment
36					
37					
38					
39					
40					
41					
42					
43					
44					
45					
45					
47					
48					
49					
50					
51					
52					
53					
54					
55					
56					
57					
58					
59					
60					
61					
62					
63					
64					
65					
66					
67					
68					
69					
70					

	Name/occupation	Phone Number	*/+	Call Date	Comment
71					
72					
73					
74					
75					
76					
77					
78					
79					
80					
81					
82					
83					
84					
85					
86					
87					
88					
89					
90					
91					
92					
93					
94					
95					
96					
97					
98					
99					
100					

Save this list in your computer or on file cards or in a notebook and keep adding to the list every time you meet anyone new!

Exercise #16b

People I can count on to encourage me are: _____

_____

_____

_____

_____

_____

_____

_____

I will look for new friends in the following places:

Church	Neighborhood Groups
Gym	Internet (be careful!)
Office	Adult Classes
Civic Meetings	Little League
Hobby Classes	School Plays/Recitals
Neighbors	Bridge Club
Library Book Clubs	Support Groups
PTA Meetings	Traveling
Volunteer Work	Conventions/Trade Shows
School Reunions	Business Socials
Part-time Jobs	Tutoring Adults
Walking/Jogging	Entrepreneurial Groups
Fundraisers	Bookstores
_____	_____
_____	_____

(I've left spaces for you to write in places I've overlooked.) Major cities across the U.S. have success seminars on a large and small scale. These are opportunities to meet and network with people who are also looking to improve themselves. Check out these seminars and attend one. Your local convention bureau or newspaper should be able to give you information.

𝕰𝕩 CHAPTER SEVENTEEN 𝕩𝕰

People Skills for Life

> *"He who can do this (win friends and influence people)*
> *has the whole world with him.*
> *He who cannot walks a lonely way."*
> –Dale Carnegie

THE IMPORTANCE OF PEOPLE SKILLS

People want to help people with whom they feel a connection. Any good salesperson will tell you that people buy from people they like. That's why people skills are paramount if you're going to reach your goal.

How do you break the ice with people you don't know? It's very common to feel awkward about going to a meeting alone, going to a party where you don't know anyone, or standing around with a lot of mothers you've never met waiting to pick up your kids at school. If you're shy about new people, remember these two steps to break the ice:

1. Smile — it opens doors faster than a key. There's a line from a song by the Eagles, "City girls seem to find out early, how to open doors with just a smile." It's almost impossible not to return a smile. Try it. It's the easiest way in the world to begin a conversation.

2. Sincerely compliment people — a simple comment like "What a lovely dress" or "You look so bright and cheery today" or "What an incredible job you did organizing that fundraiser," go a long way toward starting a friendship. Don't say it if you don't mean it, but everyone has something worthy of a compliment if you just pay attention.

Another people skill that has to be mentioned here is courtesy. In today's world in which an email replaces a thank you note and a quick bite on the run replaces sit-down lunches, we tend to forget the personal niceties of good behavior. Ours is an "in your face" society. We laugh at rudeness and perpetuate bad manners. "Me first" is our mantra. We no longer hold doors for each other or pay attention to how people should be acknowledged or introduced. "Casual Fridays" have given way to "casual manners."

Unfortunately, even while we claim not to care, down underneath it still matters. Read up on the rules of courtesy — they really are nothing more than how to show basic consideration for one another — and follow them. You'll be surprised how positively people react when you treat them as if you care.

THE FORMula FOR SUCCESSFUL CONVERSATION

"Sure," you say, "I start the conversation, but what do I say next?" In the resources section at the end of this chapter I've recommended a couple of books by networking maven Susan RoAne, one of which is totally focused on that question. Until we practice, most of us didn't know what to say next. The secret is to ask questions the other person has to answer in some detail. The magic FORMula reminds you of the topics that always work when you're trying to build a friendship bridge.

FAMILY: Are you married or single? Any children? How many? Where are you from originally? How did you come to live here? Where did you go to school? (If you're from the same city, it won't be long before you find someone you know in common.)

OCCUPATION: What do you do for a living? How did you land that job? Do you enjoy your work? Where is your office? How long have you been in this line of work?

RECREATION: What do you do for fun? How do you spend your leisure/vacation time? Have you been to (country or place of choice)? What sports do you like? What do you think of the (local team's) chances this year?

M(Your) MESSAGE: I'm making a career change...I'm in the process of starting my own business... I just started offering a new service for customers.

It's almost impossible not to find some common ground on which to start building the friendship bridge.

One warning: God gave you two ears and one mouth so you could listen twice as much as you talk. Listen to what people say and respond to what they tell you. Don't just push what you want them to know about you. You'll need to focus while you listen because the average person speaks at 100 words per minute — and listens at five times that speed!

CARE TO LISTEN

Have you ever had someone introduce themselves and tell you their name and two seconds later you can't remember what they said? It's a prime example of how self-absorbed we can be. We're usually too busy thinking of what we are going to say next to listen to what is being said to us.

To get what you want you've got to be tuned in to what others want. Most people's favorite radio station is WIIFM (What's In It For Me?). The truth is, "People don't CARE what you think, unless they think you CARE." The CARE method of listening shows you are trying to understand and are interested in what is being said.

CONCENTRATE only on the speaker. Don't look around the room as if you're checking to see if there's anyone more interesting nearby. Mary Kay Ash was known for the total attention she gave to each person who spoke to her. You felt as if there were no one else on the planet she wanted to talk to more than you.

ACKNOWLEDGE what the speaker is saying. Do this through maintaining eye contact, nodding, and making comments like "I see" or "right." Don't interrupt while the person's talking. Don't interject your opinion unless it's asked for. You're here to hear — talking comes later.

RESPOND with open-ended questions. "Tell me more about that," or "How did that affect you?" If you ask questions that can be answered with a simple "yes" or "no" you've put a period on the conversation. Watch the professional interviewers on TV and copy their style. The person asking questions is the person in control of the conversation.

EXERCISE emotional control. Listen to the other person's perspective and reasons for doing things. This isn't the time give a rebuttal or to sell your point of view. You're building bridges establishing a relationship and hopefully building a new friendship or contact as you head down the road toward your goal.

Understand your strengths and weaknesses. Expand your circle, surrounding yourself with people who can strengthen your areas of weakness. Learn from them, shamelessly soaking up all the information they have to give you. They will be your first line of defense and your best back-up all at the same time.

Suggested Resources:

Books:

How to Work a Room: The Ultimate Guide to Savvy Socializing in Person and Online by Susan RoAne. (Harper: 2000 — ISBN: 0060957859)

What Do I Say Next? - Talk Your Way to Business and Social Success by Susan RoAne. (Warner Books:1999 -ISBN: 0446674265)

Power Etiquette: What You Don't Know Can Kill Your Career, by Dana May Casperson. (AMACOM, 1999 — ISBN: 8814479987)

FIVE-MINUTE EXERCISE #17

My goal is to:_____by (date goal will be reached)_____
If I don't reach for my goal, here's how my life will look:
At home: _____

_____

At work: _____

_____

With my family: _____

_____

To my friends:_____

_____

To myself: _____

_____

&<⊱ CHAPTER EIGHTEEN ⊰>&

The Personality Rainbow

> *"Nothing in life is to be feared,*
> *it is only to be understood."*
> *–Marie Curie*

THE GOLDEN RULE IS WRONG

We all learned the Golden Rule of "Do unto others as you would like them to do unto you." This is the furthest thing from the truth when it comes to communicating with other people. Conflict management is such a hot issue today because people are simply unconsciously unaware of these basic personality types. If you don't understand the differences in people, you don't know how to communicate effectively with others. Everyone will be more receptive to your message if you address them the way *they* want you to -rather than the way you would prefer to be addressed.

READING PEOPLE IS AN ART, NOT A SCIENCE

Many years ago I learned to recognize people by their personality types and it has been invaluable in relating to new friends in ways that were comfortable for both of us. The early Greek philosophers first identified the basic four personality groups. They have been talked about ever since and today most sales trainers teach them as part of a salesperson's basic tool kit. I am a firm believer that if everyone were trained to understand these four basic personality types, we would be much more tolerant, we would have a much better understanding of each other, and we would be able to communicate easily with each other.

The point is that you want to be able to know what kind of person you're talking to. When you know how they are going to act and react, you can better judge what will interest them and what will turn them off.

WHAT COLOR ARE YOU?

While the basic personality types have been categorized as shapes, animals, colors, gems, fishes and many more, I like to use the color sorting method. While each of us has a portion of each color as part of our personality makeup, we have one dominant personality type/color. Each has strengths and weaknesses you should be able to recognize. Let's look at them one by one.

THE PASSIVES (YELLOWS) ARE "CAUSE-ORIENTED."

Yellows are emotional but they don't show it. They listen carefully to everything, usually without comment at that moment. They make great team members at work because they get the job done without complaining. They're often shy and would prefer to stay in the background so you won't find them on the cheerleading squad or running the meeting.

Yellows (Passives)

Priority: Cause-oriented.

Pace: Open, friendly, smile, walk and talk slowly

Dress: Earthtones, comfortable

Motivation: Harmony, balance, equality

Approach: Be open and friendly, talk to them at a slower pace

Turn Off: Pushy people, confrontation, conflict

Occupation: Nurse, teacher, counselor, artist, activist

Environment: Plants, trees, natural setting, open, airy

Positive traits: Loyal, team player, caring, supportive, emphathetic listener, romantic

Negative: Makes slow decisions, difficult to read, to spare feelings, risk averse

Movie: *Out of Africa*

Famous Yellows: Mother Theresa, Jane Goodall, Laura Bush

THE SOCIALS (BLUES) ARE "FUN-ORIENTED."

Blues love being around people. They are optimistic, motivating and enthusiastic. They may have a current task at hand but can quickly lose focus on a better offer — like going to the beach. They're natural persuaders and love to have people rally behind whatever cause they're involved with. They're also disorganized and often get so caught up with the today's issues that they forget to follow-through on the earlier project.

Blues (Socials)

Priority: Fun

Pace: Erratic, loud, animated, dramatic

Dress: Bright colors, showy, trendy

Motivation: Recognition, fame, fun

Approach: Be lively and open. They love to chit-chat

Turn off: Anything monotonous and boring, being alone

Occupation: Entertainer, promoter, musicians, actor, sales

Environment: Pictures of people, trophies, disorganized and cluttered desk

Positive traits: Can rally people, personable, warm, charming, high energy, enthusiastic and likeable

Negative: Poor time management, impulsive, moody, easily gets off track

Movie: *Bill & Ted's Excellent Adventure*

Famous Blues: Julia Roberts, Bette Midler, Goldie Hawn

THE ANALYTICALS (GREENS) ARE "FACT-ORIENTED."

Greens are practical and efficient. They don't make snap decisions, preferring to make pro and con lists before they make a choice. Ask them for a decision now and they'll have to get back to you. Their need for systems and perfection make them seem critical or unresponsive. Actually, if they don't react it's because they're looking at the issue from every side before offering a response.

Greens (Analyticals)

Priority: To be prepared, precise, exact and right

Pace: Slow, methodical, calculating, systematic

Dress: Practical

Motivation: Data, facts, details, wants guarantees

Approach: Be reserved, statements should be backed up with facts, documentation.

Turn off: Disorganization, loud, obnoxious people

Environment: Structured, neat, manuals, documentation

Occupation: Accountants, engineers, statisticians, programmers, architects

Positive traits: Excellent attention to detail, follow through, good problem solver

Negative: Over-analyzes, very critical, pessimistic, difficulty meeting deadlines

Movies: Any documentary, *2001 Space Odyssey*

Famous Greens: Condoleezza Rice, Lillian Vernon, Sally Ride

THE DRIVEN (REDS) ARE "CHALLENGE-ORIENTED."

Reds are assertive and want to be in control. Just try telling them they can't do something, and they'll prove you're wrong every time. They are natural multi-taskers, often biting off more than they can chew and overextending themselves. They have lots of energy and people gravitate to them because they're natural leaders. They would rather talk than listen, and they have very little patience. Things have to be done their way and they have to be done right now.

Reds (Driven)

Priority: Challenge-oriented, power, control

Pace: Impatient, fast, decisive, competitive

Dress: Sharp, tailored, brand conscious

Motivation: Results, bottom line, being number one, winning

Approach: Recognize their accomplishments, be direct and to the point, and respectful of their position and time

Turn off: Slow, indecisive people, small talk

Occupation: High level executive, government or military leader

Environment: Large desk, sits in position of power, awards & plaques on wall

Positive traits: Efficient, quick, gets the job done

Negative: Pushy, arrogant, insensitive, self-centered, self-absorbed
Movie: *Wall Street*
Famous Reds: Oprah Winfrey, Barbara Streisand, Hillary Clinton, Erin
Brockovitch

BEGIN THE SORTING PROCESS

Revisit the list of people you know and categorize them according to
these four personality types. Are you surprised how easy it is to label each
one? Do you see why you hang out with the people you do and why you
have conflicts with others? Think about how, knowing what influences
them, you would talk to them and motivate them in the future.

When you know what people like and positively react to, you have the
ability to say and do the things that will please them, compel them and move
them. Salespeople know: when the customer is pleased, the customer buys.

Can you see how these different personality types can compliment your
strengths and skills, and help you build your Champion Circle?

Julie was responsible for soliciting volunteers to run the annual auction
for a local charity. After advertising for volunteers in the community paper,
she met with the applicants at the local library to discuss the fundraising
theme and the organization's goal. Julie was schooled in the color catego-
rizing method of successful team building, so with a big smile she addressed
the crowd: "Welcome and thank you for coming to the first meeting of this
year's auction volunteers. I know you're all busy and I commend you on your
dedication to a worthy cause *(a compliment for everyone)*.

"The success of the event will depend on the team we build and the
cooperation and support from the community. This may not be for you, but
I know it will be a highly profitable and successful event *(a challenge for the
Reds)*. We are sure to get a lot of recognition and attention of many high
ranking officials as we create a party atmosphere where everyone can have a
tremendous amount of fun *(recognition and fun for the Blues)*. You can feel
good about what we are doing as the money we raise will go to expand our
youth center so we can host a variety of after-school youth programs, expand
our staff to accommodate more children in our day care program, and have
money to upgrade community play structures *(supportive and cause-oriented
for the Yellows)*. We will structure our program so each person has written
information for a thorough understanding of our fund-raising goals, the
items we will auction, the process of bidding, and how accounts will be
settled *(full details for the Greens)*."

After answering questions, Julie was happy to find a chairperson for the auction, as well as the 20 volunteers needed to co-chair the subcommittees, and plenty of volunteers to help with the details of this enormous project. Her people skills and understanding of color sorting helped make the auction a great success.

In exercise #16A I gave you an example of going through a bucket of 100 oysters to find the five pearls that were worth $5,000 each. Here's how each personality would look at this example:

- The yellow personality may want to put the oysters back in their natural habitat or just keep them alive.

- The blue personality would look for others to join in the fun. However if something better came up, they might get distracted and move on to what they perceive to be more fun.

- The greens would analyze for days the probability of there actually being any pearls among these oysters and the best possible way of determining which ones had pearls and how to open them.

- The reds would go through the bucket quickly and efficiently, finding all five.

SEE FOR YOURSELF

There are two exercises in this chapter. In the first, you will identify your primary color. By answering the questions and following the scoring directions you'll recognize your primary and secondary personality types.

Then in Part B, go back to Exercise #16A, Who You Know, and color categorize the people who you designated to be on your "A" list.

Suggested Resources:

Books:

*The Platinum Rule: Discover the Four Basic Business Personalities —
and How They Can Lead You to Success* by Anthony Alessandra
(Warner Books, 1998 — ISBN: 0446673439)

The Conative Connection: Acting on Instinct by Kathy Kolbe
(Addison-Wesley Pub Co; Reprint edition, 1997 — ISBN:
0201570955)

*The 7 Powers of Questions: Secrets to Successful Communication in
Life and at Work* by Dorothy Leeds (Perigee: 2000- ISBN:
0399526145)

FIVE-MINUTE EXERCISE #18A
Basic Personality Assessment

Answer each of the questions with one of the following responses:

0 — if the question applies to you "almost never or not at all."
1 — if the question somewhat applies to you.
2 — if the question absolutely applies to you.

Section A

___ Money and challenges are strong motivators for you.
___ To what extent do you feel motivated when faced with a challenge?
___ To what extent are you able to handle pain?
___ Do you have strong willpower?
___ Do you wear or want to wear expensive clothing or jewelry, or
  drive a luxury car?
___ How important is it to you to have everything "first class"?
___ When it comes to clothing, is style generally more important than
  comfort?

___ Do you generally like people to get to the point versus chit-chat?
___ Do you consider yourself a workaholic?
Total: ___

Section B

___ To what extent do fun and recreation motivate you?
___ Are you willing and able to perform in front of others?
___ Do you generally wear clothes embossed with names, sayings and/or logos?
___ Do you tend to attract attention to yourself?
___ How true is this statement for you: "If it tastes good, I'll eat it"?
___ People tell me I am good with people.
___ Do recreational activities involving body movement interest you?
___ Do you "live to party" and "party to live"?
___ Are you usually high-energy and enthusiastic?
___ People consider you very open, social and a warm.
Total: ___

Section C

___ My sense of compassion is a guiding force in my life?
___ Are your clothes generally more comfortable than stylish?
___ Do you live by a code of morals and ethics?
___ Are you compassionate and empathetic?
___ When choosing a car, is safety more important than style or economy?
___ Do you have great concern for the environment?
___ Do you prefer healthy foods?
___ Do you enjoy nature hikes?
___ Are you spiritual and believe in a higher consciousness?
___ Do you have difficulty saying "no"?
Total: ___

Section D

___ I enjoy reading and knowing facts and figures.
___ Do you try and control your emotions?
___ Do you enjoy intellectual games?

____ When choosing a car, is economy more important than style?
____ Are you usually aware of the time?
____ Are you impressed by efficiency and punctuality?
____ Are you very thrift and conservative?
____ Is it important that you know the reason behind a request or command?
____ Are you more introverted; prefer working alone?
____ Are order, neatness and precision important?
Total: ____

Now, add up all the points in each section, find the totals, and place A, B, C, and D in the boxes below.

Red   A _____
Blue   B _____
Yellow   C _____
Green   D _____

When you look at your totals in each box, it becomes immediately apparent which color group you fall into. The box with the highest score is your primary personality. You can see you also have numbers in the other boxes because we all have some characteristics of each color.

FIVE-MINUTE EXERCISE #18B

Go back to the list of people you made in Exercise #16A. Using what you now know about personality differences, working with your A-List people, put a color designation next to each name. Now in the boxes below, do the same thing with the five people you spend the most time with and five people with whom you work. As you meet new people, try and assign them a color as well. You'll soon see who you're most comfortable being around.

(While we often get along best with our same color type, it doesn't always work that way. For instance, two Reds may strike sparks as they jockey for control. A Blue and a Green may not be able to co-exist happily in the same meeting

room. A profit-motivated Red may not understand the cause-motivated Yellow. The more you watch people with the color chart in mind, the more you'll see the basic differences.)

My Five Closest Friends   Color
1. _____   _____
2. _____   _____
3. _____   _____
4. _____   _____
5. _____   _____

My Five Co-Workers   Color
1. _____   _____
2. _____   _____
3. _____   _____
4. _____   _____
5. _____   _____

My Family Members   Color
1. _____   _____
2. _____   _____
3. _____   _____
4. _____   _____
5. _____   _____

Others   Color
1. _____   _____
2. _____   _____
3. _____   _____
4. _____   _____
5. _____   _____

Add other people to the lists as you think of them.
(You might also color-code your family so you can make sure
Thanksgiving dinner goes smoothly this year.)

THOUGHT PROVOKER: THEY SAID IT COULDN'T BE DONE...

When you're tempted to believe the people who say you can't or won't or shouldn't, remember these opinions from recognized authorities of their days...

"Everything that can be invented has been invented."
–Charles H. Duell, Commissioner, U.S. Office of Patents, 1899

"You ain't goin' nowhere, son. You ought to go back to drivin' a truck."
–Jim Denny, manager of the Grand Ole Opry, to Elvis Presley, 1954

"We don't need you. You haven't gotten through college yet."
–Hewlett Packard to Steve Jobs, who then founded Apple Computers.

"If I had thought about it, I wouldn't have done the experiment. The literature was full of examples that said you can't do this."
–Spencer Silver on finding the adhesives for 3-M "Post-It™" notepads.

"We don't like their sound, and guitar music is on the way out."
–Decca Recording Co., rejecting the Beatles, 1962

"Who wants to hear actors talk?"
–H.M. Warner, Warner Brothers studios, 1927.

"There is no reason anyone would want a computer in their home."
–Ken Olson, president, chairman and founder of Digital Equipment Corp., 1977

"The concept is interesting and well-formed, but in order to earn better than a 'C', the idea must be feasible."
–A Yale University management professor in response to Fred Smith's paper proposing reliable overnight delivery service. (Smith later founded Federal Express.)

"I think there is a world market for maybe five computers."
–Thomas Watson, chairman of IBM, 1943

"By the turn of the century, we will live in a paperless society."
–Roger Smith, chairman of General Motors, 1986

"A cookie store is a bad idea. Besides, the market research reports say America likes crispy cookies, not soft and chewy cookies like you make."
–Response to Debbi Fields' idea for starting Mrs. Fields' Cookies.

Don't let anyone steal your dream by telling you it won't work!

❧ CHAPTER NINETEEN ☙

Do It Anyway

> *"All things are possible until they are proved impossible-even the impossible may only be so as of now."*
> *—Pearl S. Buck*

YOU HAVE TO WANT IT AND BELIEVE YOU CAN HAVE IT

Think of all the things we take for granted in this world that were once thought impossible. The list is endless. If the innovators in our civilization had listened to the skeptics, we'd still be living in caves and hunting for each day's food with spears. The reason we don't is because these men and women didn't listen when they were told their idea wouldn't work.

Have you ever heard the old saying: "They said it couldn't be done, but since she didn't hear them she went ahead and did it anyway"? There's a lot of truth to that. How many times do you think the Wright brothers were told it was stupid to believe they could make an object fly with people inside? At the beginning of the 20th century well-known physicists were saying that the theory of relativity was ridiculous and that atoms would never be harnessed for energy. Albert Einstein ignored them. As he said, "Great ideas have always received opposition from mediocre minds."

As silly as it sounds today, there was a time not so long ago when it was thought no human could run the mile in less than four minutes without having his heart burst. Then, on May 6, 1956 in New York's Madison Square Garden, Roger Bannister ran the mile in 3.59.4 seconds. The world was stunned. He had done the impossible. In 2003, the mile record stands at 3.43 seconds. Obviously, the day has to come when someone will reach a time that can't be topped, but I've never known an athlete who thought any record was unbeatable. The will to raise the bar and break it is what keeps them going.

When television finally arrived on the scene, more than 70 years after it was first conceived of, no one thought it would ever be a commercial success. Why would anyone want to have boxes in our living rooms that we sat around and watched? In the 1970s, executives questioned why anyone would ever have need for a personal computer in their home. You get the idea.

NOTHING IS IMPOSSIBLE

What was once thought impossible or improbable is today common-place. When Dick Tracy first used his wrist telephone in the comic strip, America read and smirked. It was science fiction. Now we routinely expect people to give us their cell phone number — and their email address — as part of their standard information. I have seen ads for Palm Pilots® built into wristwatches. Yesterday's impossible has become today's commonplace.

Did you see the television movie, *Door to Door?* It's the story of Bill Porter, a man who was born crippled by cerebral palsy. Bill refused to live on welfare so he talked to Watkins, a company selling household products door-to-door in the 1950s. They finally agreed to give him their worst route in Portland, Oregon and figured that's the last they'd hear from him. Through sheer tenacity and courage, he went on to become their top producing salesman not only in Portland but throughout the entire United States. Bill Porter thought of his disability not as an obstacle or setback, but as a spring-board to a positive and successful life. How do you think of whatever is holding you back?

That's why I claim that nothing is impossible. If you have an idea you believe in and the enthusiasm to sell it to others, coupled with a willingness to work against the roadblocks people will put in your path, you can make anything happen. Are you feeling better about yourself? Are you getting excited about the possibilities? Are you becoming more confident through readings these stories? You've now tapped into the world of possibilities. Your mind is open and your eyes and ears will now start to notice and hear things that could be possible avenues to achieving your goals. People will come into your life who will provide knowledge and information to help you with your vision.

It's Okay to Make Mistakes

*"If you have made mistakes …there is always another chance for you
…you may have a fresh start any moment you choose,
for this thing we call 'failure' is not the falling down,
but the staying down."*
–Mary Pickford

I guarantee that during your journey to the life of your dreams, you'll sometimes go too far out on a limb and have to reverse course for a little while, or you'll make a mistake and have to correct it, or you'll find you're spinning your wheels and have to regroup. That's fine. If you never make a mistake, you're not doing anything. But the secret is to bring enthusiasm to everything you do.

If you listen to a lot of our most popular comics today you'll notice they get their biggest laughs by being negative. They are laid back, cynical, getting the laugh with the cutting remark rather than old time slapstick. Yes, they're funny but they're also toxic. You begin to look at the world the way they do. When you're always trying to find fault and point out errors, it keeps you from finding the joy in your activities.

It's the difference between the complaints of Roseanne Barr and the madcap silliness of Lucille Ball. They both make you laugh but the over-the-top Lucy style makes you feel good. And I'd be willing to bet our grandchildren won't know who Roseanne is, but they'll still be watching *I Love Lucy.*

Another lesson Lucille Ball can teach us is to never give up. She had originally looked for a movie career. She appeared in a number of films, even had featured roles in a few of them, but as a film actress never really caught on. She thought her career was over. People were advising her to give it up. Her studio cut her from their roster.

When things were darkest, her agent suggested she make one last try — in television. Back then, television was considered one step up from oblivion but she wasn't about to give up. Maybe she could use it as a steppingstone back to the movies.

Then she met Desi Arnez, the *Lucy* show was born and the rest, as they say, is show business history.

I hope you've been thinking about what you want to do to turn your life around. In Exercise #11 you wrote out a contract with yourself, promising what you would do to make your goal a reality. Now it's time to start thinking about how you're going to achieve that.

In the next exercise, I want you to start making definite plans about your method for reaching your goals. I have given you space for three different goals. Don't be concerned if you only have one or two.

Some of you will be planning to lose weight, exercise and stop smoking. While it may be difficult to do them all at once, it's possible. So you can fill in all the lines.

Others may only want to concentrate on one thing at a time and that's fine too. As I keep stressing, this is your life and your plan and you get to choose how you do it or redo it. It seems to me that the problem with a lot of books is that they assume everyone is the same and will react identically to situations. We know that's ridiculous. We each bring different reactions to the table based on our past histories, current circumstances, and personal dreams. And it's why I encourage you to do things your way within the *Gimme Five!* Method.

The steps you'll take toward your goal can be nothing more than baby steps. You can cut down one cigarette a day. You don't have to go cold turkey. You can cut out one food. You can add one hour of reading on a money generating activity you enjoy.

These are the tiny first goals you'll meet — the first bites of that hippopotamus we talked about. If you just concentrate on the little victories, before long you'll have met the challenge and come out on top.

Suggested Resources:

Books:

Ten Things I Learned from Bill Porter by Shelly Brady, Bill Porter(Wheeler Publishing, 2002 — ISBN: 1587243512)

Unstoppable People: How Ordinary People Achieve Extraordinary Things by Adrian Gilpin. (Century:1999 — ISBN: 0712678085)

Unstoppable by Cynthia Kersey (Sourcebooks, 1998 — ISBN 1570713383)

Movies:

Bend It Like Beckham — starring Prminder Nagra, Keira Knightley and Jonathan Rhys-Meyers. The Director/co-writer, Gurinda Chadha weaves a tale of a girl trying to find her way amid family pressures to conform to Indian traditions and her own desire to follow in her idol's cleats.

Door to Door — VHS and DVD, starring William H. Macy and Kyra Sedgwick

Rudy — VHS and DVD, starring Sean Astin (True story of a young man who won't let any obstacle stand in the way of his dream of becoming a Notre Dame football player.)

October Sky — VHS and DVD, starring Jake Gyllenhaal, Chris Cooper, Chris Owen and Laura Dern. A story of a three buddies, with the help of their teacher overcome seemingly impossible odds to fulfill a vision.

Radio — Released Oct. 24, 2003, starring Ed Harris and Cuba Gooding Jr., based on events in the life of "Radio," the mentoring relationship between a high school coach and a mentally-challenged man.

EXERCISE #19
Actions and Exercises for becoming People-Smart

My first goal is to observe people:
Over the next five days, I will take these five actions to achieve it:

1. _____
2. _____
3. _____
4. _____
5. _____

My second goal is to meet someone new:
Over the next five days, I will take these five actions to achieve it:

1. _____
2. _____
3. _____
4. _____
5. _____

My third goal is to make a new friend:
Over the next five days, I will take these five actions to achieve it:

1. _____
2. _____
3. _____
4. _____
5. _____

THOUGHT PROVOKER: THEY SAID IT WOULDN'T WORK . . .

If you're still not convinced that so-called experts sometimes don't know what they're talking about, read on…

"We have been the first, and doubtless to be the last, to visit this profitless locality."
–Lt. Joseph Ives after visiting the Grand Canyon in 1861

"This 'telephone' has too many shortcomings to be seriously considered as a means of communication. The device is inherently of no value to us."
–Western Union internal memo, 1876.

"There is not the slightest indication that nuclear energy will ever be obtainable. It would mean that the atom would have to be shattered at will."
–Albert Einstein, 1932

"While theoretically and technically television may be feasible, commercially and financially it is an impossibility."
–Lee DeForest, inventor of the television tube

"Can't act, can't sing, can dance a little."
–Negative talent assessment of Fred Astaire at MGM

"I'm just glad it'll be Clark Gable who's falling on his face not Gary Cooper."
–Gary Cooper (on his decision not to take the leading role in *Gone with the Wind.*)

"I have traveled the length and breadth of this country and talked with the best people, and I can assure you that data processing is a fad that won't last out the year."
–The editor in charge of business books for Prentice Hall, 1957

"You want to have consistent and uniform muscle development across all of your muscles? It can't be done. You just have to accept inconsistent muscle development as an unalterable condition of weight training."
–Response to Arthur Jones, who solved the problem by inventing Nautilus

Trust in your own judgment when setting your goals.

CHAPTER TWENTY

Mentoring Magic

> *"In helping others, we shall help ourselves,*
> *for whatever good we give out completes the circle*
> *and comes back to us."*
> —*Flora Edwards*

FINDING YOUR TEACHER

Have you ever heard the phrase, "When the student is ready, the teacher will appear?" Unfortunately, we often either don't recognize that teacher or aren't ready when he or she arrives on our doorstep.

Once we're out of school, the teachers who come along in our life are called mentors. These are the people who open doors for us, give us advice, help us through problems, congratulate us when we're successful and give us encouragement when the going gets rough. A good mentor is one of the most precious gifts anyone can have as they try to reach their dreams.

> I obviously wasn't ready. I had a friend who was a realtor. It was he who helped me buy and sell (with a nice profit) my first duplex, and then recommended I buy my next property, either another duplex or maybe a larger four-plex. I ignored his recommendation. I never gave it a second thought.
>
> Fifteen years later, I've watched several people retire to live off their earned income from the properties he advised them to buy. Even better, they own assets worth hundreds of thousands of dollars. Why didn't I listen when he tried to advise me? I learned my lesson.

A mentor is a good teacher, a trusted counselor and guide concerned about your professional growth and willing to help you up the ladder to success. Finding and working with a mentor is perhaps the wisest and most powerful decision you can make. This experienced individual has already done what you want to do. They've already taken the arrows in the back as they've blazed new paths. They understand the challenges you face and can streamline your process by pointing out the pitfalls and how to circumvent them.

Major decisions and small subtleties crop up constantly in every success agenda. The wisdom and advice of your experienced mentor will prove to be invaluable — and can save you not only money, but years of hard work and frustration when it comes to making the critical day-to-day decisions and testing your strategy for turning your dreams into reality.

Keep your eyes open and daily people will cross your path who will provide insight and knowledge which will help you continue your journey toward your big vision. If you remain true to your mission and open to learning you'll pick up these nuggets of gold all along the way. Here's a situation where I *did* listen to my mentor.

> In high school I worked summer jobs doing secretarial work for a temp agency. Maggie said, "Josie you've got to learn word processing. Typewriters will become obsolete." How right she was! That summer I worked for a technical writer and mastered a new skill that paid handsomely as I completed my college education.

And don't think you have to limit yourself to one mentor. Truly fortunate people have two or three in different areas of their life. Treasure them because they may determine how quickly you attain your Power-Wants.

How High is Your Stack?

No matter how much you think you know, there will always be someone who knows more. That's how life works. Until you have proved your ability, be willing to learn from others. Here's a true story that explains it well.

> A woman at one of my seminars told me about a wealthy gentlemen who was willing to show her how to make a tremendous amount of money

working for him selling environmental products. Eager to learn, she was quick to comment on his method of success and make recommendations for improving his system. He sternly looked at her and asked her how much money she made?

"None yet," she replied.

"When your stack of $100 bills is as big as mine," he said, "then you can make adjustments to this system. Until then, if I or anyone else listens to you, we'll be as successful as you are — and you said you're broke."

Whether or not we've been successful in our various endeavors, humans are always ready to contribute what we consider our valuable opinion. Remember the rule about listening, not talking. When we find a mentor we admire and respect, someone who's achieved the level of success we want, it's time to humbly listen and learn. We speak up because our ego needs some stroking. My advice: Sit on your ego, get excited about your future, and pay close attention to the expert who has walked the path before you.

Another lesson I learned: Stay as close to the mentor as you can. Learning to play basketball from a pick-up game at the local gym is profoundly different from lessons with Michael Jordan. If we hear it from someone who learned it from the successful person, we really are relying on a highly diluted formula for success.

We all played the Whisper Down the Lane, also known as Telephone, when we were young. One person whispers a message and it's passed on from kid to kid. By the time it gets to the last child in the line, the message bears no relation to the original. That's what happens as adults when we get our information from other sources. Always be the first in line who hears the message undiluted.

A Josie Rule

BE CAREFUL! When you're looking for a mentor, there are a lot of fast-talking, smooth-walking, slick-looking people who can "talk the talk," but who haven't "walked the walk." They may just want to take advantage of your eagerness to learn and willingness to do whatever they suggest. Before you choose someone as a mentor or a teammate, be sure to confirm to the best of your ability who they are, what their experience has been, and what their motives are. Trust your intuition. You get a gut feel when you meet someone. Think about the times you've gone against an instinct. Did you regret it later? When we go with our gut, we usually don't go wrong.

RULES FOR MENTORS AND MENTEES

The mentor/mentee relationship should be beneficial to both people involved. The New York-based Women Unlimited, an organization specializing in development programs for women, gives the following guidelines for each person.

Mentors, those wise heads who are giving advice, should be:
- trustworthy, so you know your confidences will be kept confidential;
- able to laugh at themselves;
- capable of listening carefully so they really understand what is going on;
- able to admit her own mistakes and share her failures so you can learn from them;
- able to discuss a wide range of relevant topics; and be comfortable in giving and receiving feedback.

As a Mentee, the recipient of the advice, you should be:
- willing to keep your mentor's confidences;
- willing to speak honestly and openly about what is going on in your life and work;
- ready to look into yourself to find answers and to understand who you are and why certain things play out the way they do;
- able to admit your mistakes and be willing to talk about your failures;
- realistic about your expectations for the relationship;
- accountable for your development because, in the long run, you are the only one who can truly shape your future.

When the mentor/mentee relationship is established and works well, it can remain in place for months, years, or a lifetime. Before long, you may find yourself in both positions, checking with your mentor for advice and at the same time leading someone else along with path.

The important thing to remember is why the relationship was established. It has nothing to do with money. The mentor donates his or her time and you, in turn, donate yours to the people you mentor. It all centers around passing on the information from one generation or experience level to another. Usually, mentors are older but they don't have to be. Your mentor may be someone younger than you who has been in business longer and therefore has insights you don't have. The secret is to find someone with whom you have good rapport and mutual respect.

PICK YOUR MENTORS CAREFULLY

Can a college professor making less than six figures a year teach you how to make more than he or she does, how to become financially independent? What you will learn from that person is specialized knowledge that will help you get a job. What does that job eventually get you? How is it that so many highly educated, talented people struggle and can barely survive financially? It's a paradox that those with higher education are so highly coveted, revered and respected and still left so disillusioned financially. Higher education or pursuing a marketable skill is a minimum to financial stability and now more than ever it is clear — it is just not enough.

Look around at the people you know. Most people define wealth by material possessions. I know many people who would be defined as wealthy based on the cars they drive, the clothes they wear and the houses they live in are, quite frankly, just broke at a higher level. It's not how much you make, it's how much you keep and having what you keep make money for you so that eventually you don't have to work. Free at last!

Therefore, while a high school teacher or college professor may be a great mentor for some things, choose other mentors to show you how to earn money from what you've learned. Most successful people are mentored by men and women who are as successful or more successful than they are. It stands to reason; if you haven't done it, it's difficult to show anyone how to do it.

So investigate your mentors just as you would investigate any other major influence in your life. Choose wisely and the benefits will be yours for a lifetime.

FORM A MASTER MIND GROUP

An increasingly popular form of peer-to-peer mentoring is the Master Mind group, people who are at an equal level in a particular business or pursuit meet by conference call or over breakfast once a month to exchange ideas, discuss their problems and share their victories. They mentor each other through an open dialogue. Like any other mentor relationship, the communications are confidential but the results are spectacular. The common sharing of experiences and the opportunity to present your particular challenge to a new set of eyes results in insights that have often changed lives dramatically. When we are entangled in our own crisis, it's hard to step back and look at the problem from another dimension, let alone several dimensions. The Master Mind group allows that.

Usually, Master Mind groups are five or six people. If they get too large, they become unwieldy and too difficult to manage. In some situations, there may be a leader, a person with significantly more experience, who runs the group. In those situations, there may be more participants and the sessions are usually held on conference calls.

For our purposes, a smaller group — even two or three people to begin — works well.

If you're an independent contractor, find others in your situation. If you're working with a franchise or network marketing company, you'll have lots of people to choose from, but remember to pick only those who are serious about what they're doing and successful in doing it.

Here are some general guidelines for Master Mind groups to keep in mind:

- Set up an inflexible meeting time. It can be bi-weekly, monthly, quarterly — whatever works for you. Most groups find monthly meetings are the most effective. This meeting should be considered as important as a doctor's appointment, not to be missed for frivolous reasons.
- Determine a place to meet. An early breakfast at a back table at the pancake house works just fine. It doesn't have to be fancy. If you're meeting by phone, set a time and stick to it. For a fee, which can be split between the members or picked up by a different member

each month, you can set up a closed conference call with your local long distance provider.

- Be sure you have an agenda for each meeting. It doesn't have to be very specific, but it should include start and end times, general topic(s) to be discussed, etc. Every member should be encouraged to suggest topics.

- Make sure everyone knows beforehand what the topic will be and try to stick to it. Obviously, there will other things discussed as they come up, but try not to veer off on unproductive tangents.

- Allow time for members' individual concerns. With email, it's easy to canvass the members before the meeting and ask if there is a specific issue that someone needs to be addressed and build that into the agenda.

- While this is meant to be a no-holds-barred conversation between equals, remember the basic rules of courtesy and respect. Even when members are being brutally honest, they need to refrain from profanity, name-calling, and put-downs.

- Never betray a confidence. What happens in the group stays in the group. This is vital to its success.

As in any other similar situation, the Master Mind group may have a fluctuating membership. I know of cases where the group has stayed together as a unit for a decade, and others where the membership has turned over completely within a few years. However it works for you, the benefits of a Master Mind meeting are almost always positive and rewarding.

BUILDING YOUR MENTOR/MASTER MIND GROUP

In Exercise #20, I want you to go through your list of people from Chapter 16, Exercise #16A. Pick out those who you think would be good mentors for you in a one-to-one relationship.

After you have your list assembled, begin to contact these people. Don't be discouraged if some turn you down. Some may already be in mentoring relationships and may not have time for another. Some may not feel comfortable in that role. Keep contacting people until you find your first mentor.

Then make another list of those who would be effective in a Master Mind group. Next to each name, identify the skill that person may be able to teach you or what experience that person has that will help you make decisions that will help your reach your goals. Don't expect these relationships to develop overnight. There will be a birth and growth cycle, but if you keep looking for those who can help you, I guarantee you'll find them.

SUCCESS TECHNIQUE #4
Participation in a Championship Circle meeting or phone call weekly will greatly increase your ability to focus, learn and produce and earn.

Suggested Resources:

Books:
Mentoring: A Success Guide for Mentors and Protégés by Floyd Wickman and Terri Sjodin. (McGraw-Hill: 1997 — ISBN: 0786311355)

Coaching and Mentoring for Dummies by Marty Brounstein (For Dummies:2000 — ISBN: 0764552236)

Movies:
These films are just a sampling of the hundreds that depict the mentor relationship.

Wit — 2001 — E.M. Ashford (Eileen Atkins) mentors Vivian Bearing (Emma Thompson)

Harry Potter and the Sorcerer's Stone — 2001 — Rubeus Hagrid (Robbie Coltrane) mentors Harry Potter (Daniel Radcliffe)

Finding Forrester — 2000 — William Forrester (Sean Connery) mentors Jamal Wallace (Rob Brown)

The Karate Kid — 1984 — Kesuke Miyagi (Pat Morita) mentors Daniel LaRusso (Ralph Macchio)

Gimme Five! Exercise #20

The following people would be great personal mentors for me:
Name: Skill-Set or Experience:

_____

_____

_____

_____

_____

_____

_____

_____

_____

_____

_____

The following people would be effective members of a Master Mind group:

_____

_____

_____

_____

_____

_____

_____

_____

_____

Never stop adding to your lists for both individual mentoring and Master Mind possibilities. It may take several tries to find just the right people for your particular situation, but they are there and you'll be glad you took the time to discover them. Along your journey there will be several companions along the way, some will be with you a short time and some will be with you through the end.

Section V:
Become Options-Smart

GIMME FIVE! RULE NUMBER FIVE

"You have only one option —
the option to do something now."

ᚳᚷ CHAPTER TWENTY-ONE ᚷᚲ

Quitting is Not an Option

"You may be disappointed if you fail,
but you are doomed if you don't try."
—Beverly Sills

FAILURE NURTURES SUCCESS

It's downright frightening to consider how dumb you'll look to your friends and family and co-workers if you take off on this new life plan of yours, and you don't show outstanding success. Gasp! You might even fail. Goodness me! How embarrassing would that be?

Frankly, not very. Failure is part and parcel of success and it always has been. There's an often-told story about Thomas Edison who invented the light bulb, among other things. He tried over 99 (or 999, depending on who's telling the story) different methods to make a light bulb and failed and failed every time at a total cost of two million dollars. Finally, he figured out how to put light in a glass bulb. A newspaper reporter asked him how it felt to have failed so often. Edison replied, "I didn't fail. I just found lots of ways not to make a light bulb."

In school a lot of us heard the story of Robert Bruce leading the Scottish rebels against the English king. He was tired and defeated. His troops weren't strong enough to contend with the larger English army. Devastated by his failure, he took refuge in a cave to get some rest and perhaps a new perspective. Thinking about his failure, he watched a spider spinning a web. The little arachnid hurled itself across the space between two rock outcroppings. Time after time it leaped and missed, necessitating a climb up the silk string back to its starting place. No matter how many times the spider tried, it always missed, although by shorter and shorter margins. Finally, long after it would have been expected to give up, the spider made it, anchored the silk, and continued weaving the web.

The message for Robert Bruce works for us today just as it worked for him in 1298. Failure doesn't matter. The important thing is not to quit. No matter how many times you fail, if you keep on trying, you'll make it — or you'll find another path that works even better.

THE FIVE REASONS PEOPLE QUIT

1. They compare themselves to others and feel inadequate. Be concerned with your goals and what you have to do to get there. Run your race at your pace and in your time.
2. In making mistakes (sometimes very costly), we become discouraged and embarrassed. Learn from your mistakes and persevere. Lasting success come rarely on the first attempt.
3. They become overly concerned with other people's opinion and criticism. Most successful people are positive and are supportive of your success. You have to live your life, pay your bills and take care of your family. If they don't contribute, they have no word in the matter. Don't get advice from people who don't have what you want and haven't done what you want to do.
4. Distractions, distractions and more distractions. Other people, other things and other opportunities tempt us to change directions and manipulate our time. Perhaps the grass looks greener on the other side. Pick a horse and ride it to the finish, keeping your goals in check along the way.
5. Fear and doubt. Build your belief by changing your thoughts, increasing your knowledge and moving forward taking steps to increase your confidence.

So many people quit for the above reasons, and that is why there is so much room at the top.

In a survey conducted by the National Retail Dry Goods Association found:

48% of all salespeople make one call and stop

25% of all salespeople make two calls and stop

15% of all salespeople make three calls and stop

12% go back and back and back and make 80% of all the sales.

Success Is in the Trying

Never be ashamed if you need to fall back and "regroup." Football teams do it regularly. So do armies and successful businesses. The situation is always changing and you have to be able to adapt your game plan to those changes. But the vital factor is that you don't throw in the towel. As long as you keep going, even if it means doing some broken-field running, zigzagging from here to there to get to the goal, you'll win the game.

The authors of the Chicken Soup for the Soul™ series, Jack Canfield and Mark Victor Hansen, are good examples of this. They sent their first Chicken Soup book to dozens of publishers and every one of them turned it down. But they weren't about to quit. They sent it out one more time, to a small, struggling publisher in Florida. The publisher accepted the book, without any great hopes for it. The authors promoted it without any big sales. Then a warehouse club bought it and skids of the book were delivered to their locations throughout the country. That sale triggered a mention on *The New York Times* bestseller list. Today the authors are multi-millionaires who continue to work hard to promote their product.

Because they wouldn't accept failure, they are benefiting from one of the most lucrative series in the history of publishing. You probably have read at least one of the Chicken Soup books … you and tens of millions of other people. Talk to either of Jack Canfield or Mark Victor Hansen and they'll say what I'm saying, "No matter what, never accept defeat. Learn from your failures what you're doing wrong — then fix it and try again."

"There are no secrets to success. It is the result of preparation, hard work, and learning from failure."
–Colin Powell

In Exercise #19, think back over your life and remember the things you failed at. We all had them. Maybe you didn't get a spot on the cheerleading team. Or you flunked your driver's test the first time you took it. Or you didn't get the job of your dreams. What did you do afterward? What was your reaction? What should it have been so you could learn from your mistake and do better?

When you see what you've done in the past, you will know in the future how to change your behavior, correct your course, and try again. This time you just may make it!

Suggested Resources:

Books:

Chicken Soup for the Woman's Soul by Jack Canfield (Editor), Mark Victor Hansen, Marci Shimoff, Jennifer Hawthorne (Editor) (Health Communications, 1996 — ISBN: 1558744150) There is also a second book of inspirational women's stories.

Chicken Soup for the Unsinkable Soul — Stories of Triumphing Over Life's Obstacles by Jack Canfield (Editor), Mark Victor Hansen, Heather McNamara (Health Communications, 1999 — ISBN: 1558746986)

EXERCISE #21

Reviewing your past actions and reactions is "failing forward." Your feelings of defeat and disappointment are temporary as you are learning. The day will soon come when you'll put that knowledge and wisdom to use as you move ahead accomplishing greater things.

I failed at_____
My reaction was _____
_____
I should have_____
_____
I learned that _____
_____
_____

I failed at_____
My reaction was _____
_____
I should have_____
_____
I learned that _____
_____
_____

I failed at_____
My reaction was _____
_____
I should have_____
_____
I learned that _____
_____
_____
_____
_____

THOUGHT PROVOKER: DON'T QUIT!

When things go wrong as they sometimes will,

When the road you're trudging seems all up hill,

When funds are low and the debts are high,

And you want to smile, but you have to sigh,

When care is pressing you down a bit,

Rest, if you must, but don't you quit!

Life is queer with its twists and turns

As every one of us sometimes learns,

And many a failure turns about

When she might have won had she stuck it out.

Don't give up though the pace seems slow

You may succeed with another blow.

Success is failure turned inside out -

The silver tint of the clouds of doubt -

And you never can tell how close you are,

It may be near when it seems so far.

So stick to the fight when you're hardest hit

It's when things seem worst that YOU MUST NOT QUIT.

Author Unknown

𝕲 CHAPTER TWENTY-TWO 𝕾

Your Path and Purpose

> *"It's not so much how busy you are, but why you are busy. The bee is praised; the mosquito is swatted."*
> —Marie O'Connor

We've spent a lot of time looking at the mindset behind the *Gimme Five!* Method. By this point, you should be full of resolve and eager to get started on the process of turning your life around.

I want to concentrate on things you can do to achieve your goals. I'm going to assume that if your vision is concerned with physical issues — weight, bad habits, exercise, attitude, lifestyle — you probably know what you need to do. *Gimme Five!* gives you a way to do it, a method for segmenting your dreams into achievable bites.

However, if your vision includes the need for money and the desire to be self-sufficient, even wealthy, then this is what you've been waiting for. For decades the formula of earning your degree and then working forty years for a "good company" was all you needed to feel successful. Today's message is, "Hedge, baby, hedge."

With mergers, consolidation, unemployment, recession, and the dot-com bust at the turn of the century, today's employees realize "job security" is an unattainable myth.

In previous exercises, you've had the opportunity to examine your likes and dislikes, skills and interests, so you may already have an idea what you can look at as a way to increase your income and riches.

Now, let's get specific so you know where you're heading and how you're going to get there. What are you going to do to have money flowing in the door. Will you continue to earn a linear income (You work, you get paid. You don't work, you don't get paid). Will you put the money you have toward an opportunity that generates a monthly positive cash flow possibly through real estate or will you look to build a business that starts earning residual income?

Not everyone understands residual income. It's money that's generated without you doing anything on an ongoing basis. Book royalties, stock dividends, software license fees, rental income … these are all residual income. You do the original work and the product continues to generate income on a regular basis. Most of us choose residual income as the best option of all.

WHAT'S HAPPENING?

We've spent a lot of time talking about things you can do and should do and might want to do and probably have to do. What we haven't discussed is:

WHAT ARE YOU GOING TO DO TODAY?

The old Nike shoe slogan is over-quoted but it was so on target: "Just Do It!" It's time to stop thinking, preparing, discussing, wondering, pretending, planning and all the other procrastinating activities we can think up.

The motivational speakers call it "paralysis by analysis." It's easy to get so caught up in the preparations that we never get to the party. We are so cautious about planning for every eventuality that we never take the first step toward our dream.

By this time, you should have some idea what you want to do to change your life.

- Are you going to start a new career?
- Will you provide a product or service?
- Will you find a future in sales?
- Is the franchise route the best one for you?
- Is the *Gimme Five!* Method going to be used to make you more

money — or change your living situation — or develop new, healthy habits while dropping the old ones?

- Do you have your Future Book filled out and are you adding to it regularly?
- Have you identified your Power-Wants and written them down?
- Have you assembled your support team?
- Have you looked at your finances and planned for better money management in the future?
- What have you done today to move ahead?
- What are you going to do tomorrow? And the next day? And the next?

FINANCIAL OPTIONS

The April 15, 2003 issue of *Family Circle* reported on their national survey of 3,315 men and women. Based on reader responses in January, 2003, 64 percent of Americans say they are living paycheck to paycheck, including 49% of those with income of $50,000 to $99,999. More amazing, 24% of those with incomes of $100,000 or more are in the same situation. If just one spouse lost their job, they would have to file for bankruptcy within three months.

This survey and the Thought Provoker in Section I, "Your Future," just underlines the need to improve your financial picture.

WHAT OPTIONS DO YOU HAVE?

These are just a few ways for you to make more money now and use that money as a tool to work for you so you can live a life you've dreamed of and achieve financial independence.

1.   Further your education.

The Motley Fools publish wonderful books on money. One of my favorites is the book written for teens but a marvelous resource for any age. In it they talk about the earning power of education and show that a college graduate, at a minimum, will earn at least twice what a high school graduate will make. Of course, as the degrees pile up, the earning difference widens.

This doesn't mean if you don't have a degree you can't do anything. Your first option is to get one. Remember Rose who went to college in her eighties! What's stopping you? There are community colleges, night schools, trade schools, and you can even get your degree over the Internet.

> *"People with a college degree earn on average 81% more than those with only a high school diploma. As of 2003, the gap in earnings potential over a lifetime between a high school graduate and someone with a bachelor degree is more than one million dollars." –The College Board*

Another misconception is that you have to go to one of the Ivy League or Big Ten universities. Phooey. State schools turn out all sorts of very wealthy Americans. Warren Buffet, the second richest man in the U.S. (next to Bill Gates) went to the University of Nebraska, as did Johnny Carson. Oprah Winfrey, Katie Couric and David Letterman all went to state schools.

The most important factor is not the exclusivity of the school but the quality of the student. If you really want to learn, almost any school can teach you what you need to know. The important thing is to keep learning!

2. Work more hours or get a higher paying job.

This is at best a good temporary fix. You can always make money, you can never regain your time. Is the sacrifice worth the effort? Attaining a college degree requires a significant investment of both time and money, however your potential is significantly enhanced once you can apply your knowledge toward a developing career. However, in any job your boss ultimately controls your income. Think about this: How high in the company can you really go? There are few positions at the top, with stiff competition and nasty politics to overcome if you are to get there. Instead, you continue to plod along, making the company owner or stockholders rich.

How secure are you? Company loyalty is a thing of the past. Just remember these business horror stories.

- For 50 years IBM had a no-layoff policy. In 1992 and 1993 they quickly adopted one and shaved the payroll by 120,000 people.
- Netscape was formed in 1994, went public in 1995, and by 1999

was purchased and absorbed by America Online.

- Arthur Andersen LLP was one of the Big Seven international accounting firms hiring only the best and the brightest college graduates. Today the company is virtually gone, its employees scattered to other firms — if they could find work. The Andersen website is reduced to one page which gives the address of the Chicago home office — but there may not be anyone to answer the phone.

- Enron Corporation, which brought down Arthur Anderson, stripped its workforce not only of jobs but of pension plans, stock investments, and life savings. The CEO, Ken Lay, and other top executives walked away with millions.

- A leader in the cash rich telecommunications industry, WorldCom laid off 17,000 workers in April, 2002. In 2003, along with United Airlines, Kmart, and dozens of other companies, they sought bankruptcy protection. (K-Mart came out of bankruptcy in 2003 but only after they had closed 323 stores and laid off over 32,000 workers.)

- The major telecommunications companies permanently cut 70,000 workers in 2002, while another 40,000 were laid off in 2003. Verizon has cut 22,000 jobs. Sprint has cut 2100 workers.

- The dot-com craze at the end of the 1990s saw teenagers become multi-millionaires over night and established CEOs drop everything to hop on the bandwagon. When the bubble burst after 2000, a huge percentage of dot-coms were out of business seemingly overnight and the instant millionaires had become instant paupers.

Here's the point I'm trying to make: If you work for someone else, you are susceptible to the fallout from problems created by other people's mismanagement and malfeasance. When you work for yourself, you alone must bear the burden and take the blame, but you also celebrate all the victories and grab the acclaim because you're the only one in charge.

3. Evaluate self-employment careers in sales, real estate, finance, insurance.

These choices allow you to work independently, have flexibility in your schedule and earn high incomes through sales and ongoing commission.

Remember, here you are solely responsible for your income and if anything happens to you, your income is jeopardized.

In their book *The Millionaire Next Door,* authors Thomas Stanley and William Danko, found two-thirds of their sampling were self-employed. What's more, the entrepreneurs were four times more likely to be millionaires than those who worked for others. And according to a 1999 Lou Harris survey, of the one thousand self-employed Americans and small entrepreneurs, nine out of ten stated money was not their top motivator. It was being independent and having the ability to set their own priorities that drove them.

4. Start or buy a business.

You won't have a boss but you will find yourself controlled by your customers. You will work a lot of hours, wearing a lot of hats, meeting with customers, selling your product or service, handling accounting functions, customer service issues and administrative duties. If anything happens to you, your income is jeopardized.

Kathy contacted companies for small jobs such as stuffing envelopes or filing to bring in extra money to support the family of nine. She was so professional and diligent about her work her reputation flourished and she needed to solicit help from other moms to help her keep up with the work. Kathy business grew to provide product demonstrators for a national chain of stores and was listed as one of the Inc. 500 fastest growing privately held companies. Ten years later, she sold her business for over ten million dollars.

Buying an existing business or purchasing a franchise can be costly, in the neighborhood of $10,000 to over $1,000,000. The price reflects your purchase of a recognized name and proven system of success. Buying a business can cost more than starting one. Both have risk but if you pay more to buy one and it does poorly, you have more to risk. There's a reason why a business is for sale. Is it profitable; are sales declining; does it require a significant amount of time to run? There could be market conditions or changes that are unfavorable, such as cost to product the product going up or a lease which will be increased which inevitably affects the bottom line. There's just no substitute for research, investigation and planning.

The strategy of buying a proven franchise is much more effective than going to the school of hard knocks. The McDonald's Corporation blueprint to success is undisputed. Many people do not know that in the beginning days of franchising, no one had really figured out how to make it succeed on a consistent basis and were therefore attacked mercilessly by the media and almost every state attorney general in the U.S. condemned the new business model. Some congressmen tried to outlaw franchising entirely. McDonald's turnkey franchise business and extensive training program at "Hamburger University" turned the public perception around. You can leverage your ability to learn and experience with the collective years of learning and experience of others increasing your success and reducing your stress and frustration.

Be prepared for the hours, employee issues and the realistic time it will take to see a profit, along with all the other expected issues involved in running a business.

Look for a business that caters to the masses. Bill Gates of Microsoft is a billionaire today because he bought someone else's operating system, which runs on the majority of computers in the world. Franchises like Burger King or Dunkin Donuts are universally recognized and when you buy a franchise, you pay top dollar for that recognition and the company support.

Think about how you can possibly duplicate your efforts by hiring other people to do work and bill your customers to make a profit.

> Tina started a business giving dance lessons. By her second year in business, she had three people that work for her part-time teaching grade school students after classes. Employing the efforts of other people has allowed her to generate more money without having to work more hours. She has effectively duplicated her efforts and can continue to earn an income even when she isn't working on the dance floor.

Nine in 10 companies fail in the first five years. Of those that survive, nine in 10 will fail over the next five years as well. If you insist on starting your own business, keep your day job or have sufficient funds to keep operations running until you become profitable.

5. Become an independent contractor.

Bookkeepers, writers, graphic artists, virtual assistants, web designers, and many more are taking their skills home and hiring out their expertise. Those who are independent, working full-time earn an average of 15% more than their corporate counterparts — and these independent professionals are twice as likely to have incomes in excess of $75,000 per year!

Network marketing is an ideal business with low start-up costs, no inventory to produce, warehouse or distribute, no employees and someone else to handle marketing, accounting and customer service issues. What about the ability to build a team of independent representatives who have a loyal customer base that purchases every month, and you get paid a portion of everything they order every month? Network marketing has become a choice for many entrepreneurial executives and professionals.

Take advantage of the tax laws that favor part-time or full-time home-based business. Those with a home-based business can deduct, with the proper documentation, their business vacations, their cars, meals with colleagues and much more. According to Sandy Botkin, lawyer and C.P.A., former IRS Special Agent and President of the Tax Reduction Institute, home-based business owners can set up a pension plan that makes any government program seem paltry. If your home-based business operates at a loss in the first few years, you can use that tax loss against your income.

These as just a few of the choices you have. There are hundreds more within them.

ASSETS THAT INCREASE IN VALUE

After you figure out how you're going to make more money, be sure to put your money to work for you. Invest in assets that go up in value. A brand new car loses 20% of its value the minute you drive it off the showroom floor, which is why most wealthy people buy used cars. Here are some ways you can put your money to work for you.

1. Invest in real estate.

Real estate allows you to leverage. You can purchase a property of $10,000 to $1,000,000 with only 10 to 20 percent down. There are different strategies, from buying foreclosures and fixer-uppers to buying income producing multi-units that generate monthly cash flow to assembling a team to build and buy large commercials projects. (I spent 20 years successfully working and owning my own business, yet in the five years that I've invested in real estate I've more than tripled my income)

2. Invest in the stock market.

With a 60-year history, the stock market has averaged an annual 11% return. Get the education you need to make informed, non-emotional decisions. The Internet is an incredible tool for research. Online services provide you with company background, fundamental and technical analysis and historical data. Brokerage houses often give free informational classes to help you understand how to invest your money with the hope you'll establish an account with them.

In my area, there's a weekend financial radio program hosted by Bob Brinker. I enjoy his information and learning from listeners who call in with a variety of questions. *Wall Street Week* on PBS is another favorite. Check your local radio and television stations for finance programs.

Never take anyone's suggestion of a choice "stock pick of the month" without doing lots of independent research. Always check an adviser's credentials and background. The Securities and Exchange Commission's Web site at www.sec.gov/investor/brokers.htm or the Certified Financial Planner's site at www.cfp.net list those who have faced disciplinary action.

Everyone has or knows someone that has an investment nightmare story. Hot stock tips are everywhere from the company water cooler to the weekend cocktail party and there are all too many "advisors" eager to take your money and invest it in the "flavor of the week stock." Learn the investment language. At first it can seem quite daunting, but if you take it slow and steady you can implement a simple strategy by investing in the market for the long term (at least ten years). You can start with as little as a $100 investment in companies with strong product offerings, market position, management and cash. Time and patience is a critical element.

In the *Motley Fool's Investment Guide for Teens,* they tell the story of one investor who proved that time and patience are an unbeatable combination.

In 1932, when Ann Scheiber was 38, she turned over most of her life savings to her brother, a young Wall Street stockbroker. His brokerage firm went bankrupt and Anne lost her entire investment. By 1944, she had saved $5000 and tried again, investing it all in the stock market. Ann stuck with the big trademark companies like Pepsi, Chrysler, and Coca-Cola. Instead of spending her dividends, she reinvested them in additional shares of stock. The picture wasn't always rosy. The companies experienced down years. The market went through tough periods, to the point of losing nearly half its value In 1973–1974. President Nixon resigned. The United States Armed Forces were defeated in Vietnam. Through it all, Ann held on to her investments. When she died in 1995 at the age of 101, her $5000 nest egg had grown to $22 million, which she left to New York's Yeshiva University.

Maybe you think "It can't happen now" or "I don't want to wait 50 years to become a millionaire." It *can* happen today and you don't have to wait until you've accumulated $20 million. Perhaps $5 million would suit you and you won't need to wait 50 years.

If you take $100, invest it and earn 10% per year, at the end of one year you have earned $10 in interest and now have a grand total of $110. Now you've got $110 invested at 10% and at the end of year two you have $121. At the end of year five, it will have grown to $146. At the end of year 10, it'll be worth $236. Remember, all you have invested up to this point is $100 and now at the end of year 50, you have $10,672. What if you start with more money and continue to add more money each month?It's worth your time to learn more, devise a plan and stick with it to achieve your financial goals.

3. Investing in start-up companies.

My husband and I were invited to meet with a group of investors who listened to presentations and evaluate new start-up companies seeking "seed" money to fund their existence until they became profitable and went public or were bought out. Investors discussed the proposals before them and analyzed the probability of success and made decisions to invest. Some proved quite lucrative returning up to 100 times an investor's initial investment while others never materialized. This sort of investment was central to the dot-com collapse at the turn of the century. To say it's "highly speculative and dangerous" severely understates the risk.

4. Become a private lender.

There are people who can't secure a loan for various reasons. For example, a bank will typically lend only up to 80% of the value of a home and the buyer needs to put 20% down. If the buyer only has 10%, you can be a private money lender who loans the other 10% and you can charge interest on your loan which is paid back on monthly installments and is secured by the property.

5. The next big thing.

There will always be another big invention, discovery or trend. Business, real estate and the stock market run in cycles, and there will be another successful wave and another downturn. Will you be ready? Will you recognize it and will you capitalize on it?

The important issue is that you do something to start you on the road to realizing your dreams. It may be at a job at first, but more likely it'll be doing something in which you're relatively independent.

THE REAL ESTATE OPTION

The stock market goes up and down. Companies close with little notice. But people always need a place to live and a place to work. If you invest in income-producing property — like apartment buildings or houses you can rent out or business structures — you can provide those places. You must be prudent in making these decisions, the timing, location and price you pay are major factors in determining your cash flow and immediate and long term investment success.

I often hear women say, "I never was very good in math. There's no way I could handle real estate deals." That C- in Mrs. Haye's 8th grade arithmetic class is no longer a consideration. Every form you need is available online or in computer programs. You type in the numbers. The machines spit out the figures you need.

As for complicated formulas, with income property all you have to know is:

Income, minus vacancy, minus expenses equals net income.
Net income minus the mortgage cost equals cash in your pocket.

It's pretty simple, really. You can learn enough to get you started — and to see if you like it — in classes given by your local community college or by real estate brokers in your area. There are dozens of books available.

I have recommended books throughout these chapters by Danielle Kennedy. She is one of the nation's foremost real estate trainers and a great example for all of us. She got started in real estate to help support her family. She dragged her babies with her to appointments. She learned on-the-go between diapers and PTA meetings and finding sitters. She got married at 18 but she went back to college in her thirties and has earned a couple of post-graduate degrees. She has built a wonderful life, a successful company, and an envied reputation in the real estate field. When you read what she has to say, you know you're getting the straight scoop from one of us who has been there and done that brilliantly.

Did I mention that Danielle did all this with a family of eight children? Try telling her "it can't be done."

* * * * * * * * * *

Sandy was a stay at home mom for eight years. Her husband was a highly educated and experienced CPA earning over $100K annually, eight years into his career. Because of the high cost of Bay Area living, Sandy decided to go back to work. She started as a loan agent for a local bank. Without a college background or previous real estate or mortgage experience, Sandy was able to exceed her husband's salary in her first year. With the extra earnings, they invested in income-producing properties that will eventually enable them, if they choose, to quit working and maintain their same lifestyle.

You might also think about getting a couple of people together to participate with you so you can put together bigger deals. Again, be careful. Be sure you know who you're dealing with and whether they can be trusted. My advice is to get all the education you can, find a mentor who is willing to teach you what he or she knows, and proceed with caution. You'll find the payoff is well worth the effort.

WARNING!

Never invest a cent without before talking to financial and real estate professionals to make certain the deal is suitable. Until you are very sure what you are doing, get the help you need. It's available to you.

There is no way to tell you all the ins and outs and secrets of real estate investing in this small book. I do encourage you to look into it as a source of residual income. I have listed a number of resources that will give you a wealth of information.

THE NETWORK MARKETING OPTION

In addition to real estate, I spent many years in network marketing (NM), back when it was referred to as Multi-Level Marketing (MLM).

Network marketing is simply a form of sales and distribution which takes the product to consumers through their network of friends and acquaintances. It's like the old days of door-to-door selling multiplied by thousands and increasingly handled by phone and Internet. As you sell products, you can introduce others into the business to sell product and to bring more reps into the business under them. You, at the head of this expanding network of independent distributors, get a small piece of everyone else's sales. That keeps happening even if you stop actively working the business.

How much you have to invest initially and how big the payback is differs from company to company and it's something you want to look at very carefully. The initial investment can be as low as $29 or as high as several hundred dollars. There will also be a yearly resigning fee that is usually minimal. There are NM companies in which you can make a lot of money in a relatively short time, one to two years, and others that take many years before they pay out. Here again, you need to do your homework.

The companies that we have all heard of include Amway, and their Internet spin-off, Quixtar, Arbonne, Avon, and Mary Kay Cosmetics, NuSkin, Discovery Toys, and Usana. These have been in business long enough that their excellent reputations are well deserved. If you check the MLM Woman website (www.mlmwoman.com) you'll find a list of network marketing companies they have determined are paying off for their reps.

It's a numbers game. The more people you talk to, the more people you work with, and the more people who see your products, the more successful you will be.

In very special cases, you may sponsor the person who sets the world on fire. That's every NM rep's dream. The direct marketing folklore is full of stories of millionaires who never did much but sponsor the one person who was determined to achieve his or her dream and who swept their up-line to the heights ahead of them.

In reality, you will work a lot harder and longer than you'll be told you have to, but your earning power is unlimited. It is possible to make $10 thousand a month — or $30 thousand or more. I know. I've done it. It was exciting, heady, and very satisfying.

In 1995, I started as a distributor with a new MLM company. I expected to do well because I had succeeded with another company years earlier, a company that went down in flames and took our bank account with it. At this point, I was buying things my husband and I and our small son needed by haunting neighborhood garage sales with pockets of quarters.

I threw myself into the new venture. My husband, ever patient, spent his every off-work hour caring for our son or running the other errands we needed done while I worked the business. I talked to every person I could find. I spoke to groups of 10, and then 100. Finally I was doing training for the company in front of 1000 people. My biggest crowd was 10,000 reps at the company meeting in Baltimore, Maryland. By then I was a regional vice-president and had the license plates to prove it!

During this time, I had a second child, moved to a bigger house, and somehow kept it all together. Why did I work so hard? Because I knew that the return for a relatively short time devoted to my business would result in long time financial security.

ARE YOU A SALESPERSON?

A sales career is a people intense business. You're constantly meeting new people and being rejected by a lot of them. You have to have a glad hand, a thick skin, and a passion for what you're doing. Being an independent salesperson is even harder because you have no one but yourself to motivate you. Perhaps anyone can be taught to sell, but only certain people will enjoy it. It's not for everyone. If you're one of the lucky ones who meet the criteria, your earning potential is unlimited.

In Exercise #22, I have given you a list of statements. Answer them truthfully. When you total up your replies, you'll have a pretty good indication whether or not you're a candidate for money making opportunities that require you to meet, greet, and sell to virtual strangers.

If you think a career in sales isn't for you, don't be discouraged. Sometimes it's a matter of mindset. Each of us sells everyday without realizing it. We convince someone to do us a favor, give us a new position, higher wage, begin a new relationship. We offer our services for a fee. We sold our employer on hiring us. If you like communicating with people and can learn to accept the non-personal rejection, give sales a try. You can potentially earn a substantial amount of income through commissions by which you can start turning those dreams into reality by using the income as a tool to make you money through passive, residual income

Suggested Resources:

Books & Websites:

The Best Home Businesses for the 21st Century: The Inside Information You Need to Know to Select a Home-Based Business That's Right for You by Paul Edwards, Sarah Edwards(J. P. Tarcher: 3rd edition: 1999 — ISBN: 0874779731)

Free Agent Nation:How America's New Independent Workers Are Transforming the Way We Live, by Daniel H. Pink (Warner Books, Inc., 2001 — ISBN 0-446-52523-5)

Tax Advantages for Your Home Based Business by Sandy Botkin. Sandy Botkin, President of the Tax Reduction Institute and former special counsel to the IRS.

Real Estate:

How to List and Sell Real Estate: Executing New Basics for Higher Profits, by Danielle Kennedy, et al. (South-Western College Publishing, 2002 — ISBN: 0324187769)

Seven Figure Selling: Proven Secrets to Success from Top Sales Professionals, by Danielle Kennedy (South-Western College Publishing, 2002 — ISBN: 0324187513)

How to List and Sell Real Estate Successfully, by Barb Schwarz (South-Western College Publishing, 1995 — ISBN: 0324139659)

Investments:

Jonathan Pond offers sane and sensible financial guidance. www.jonathanpond.com

The Motley Fools Investment Guide for Teens: 8 Steps to Having More Money than Your Parents Ever Dreamed Of, by David Gardner, Tom Gardner, Selena Maranjian. (Fireside: 2002 — ISBN: 0743229967)

The Women's Institute for Financial Education has been in existence since 1988 giving down-to-earth information to help women handle their money. www.wife.org

The Intelligent Investor, by Benjamin Grahm and Jason Zweig (HarperCollins Publisher Revised 7/2003 ISBN: 006055661). Over one million copies sold, The greatest investment advisor of the Twentieth Century, Benjamin Graham teaches and inspires people.

Rich Dad, Poor Dad, What The Rich Teach Their Kids About Money — That The Poor And Middle Class Do Not, by Robert Kiyosaki and Sharon Lechter (Warner Books, 3/2002 ISBN: 0446677450)

MLM Marketing:

The New Professionals, The Rise of Network Marketing as the Next Major Profession, by Charles King, James Robinson and Richard Poe (Prima Publishing; 2000 — ISBN: 0761519661)

Wave 4: Network Marketing in the 21st Century, by Richard Poe (Prima Publishing; 1999 -ISBN: 0761517529)

How to Build a Multi-Level Money Machine by Randy Gage (Gage Research & Development Inst., 1998 — ASIN: 1884667147)

MLM Woman Newsletter (Linda Locke, Editor/Publisher — Linda at: regent@west.net) Regent Press, 2081 N. Oxnard Blvd. #251, Oxnard, CA 93030 www.mlmwoman.com

www.mlm.com — provides articles, news and tools for those evaluating or involved in the mlm industry.

Gimme Five! Exercise #22

Would you be a good candidate for sales, real estate or network marketing? They require many of the same skills. Check off the answers to the following questions honestly and see if you'll do well in a "people intense" business.

Y __N__ I like to be around people.
Y __N__ I enjoy meeting new people.
Y __N__ I easily explain my ideas to others.
Y __N__ I like being in social situations with new people.
Y __N__ I usually recommend things I like to my friends.
Y __N__ have excellent organizational skills.
Y __N__ I want to run my own business.
Y __N__ I am willing to put in whatever hours are necessary for success.
Y __N__ I can learn new ways of working.
Y __N__ I enjoy teaching what I know to others.
Y __N__ I am willing to start and be responsible for my business.
Y __N__ I have high energy levels.
Y __N__ I find it easy to be enthusiastic.
Y __N__ I think it's essential to have personal and financial freedom.
Y __N__ I am willing to go to meetings and continue learning.
Y __N__ I am ready to spend time now to earn dollars later.
Y __N__ I can accept rejection without taking it personally.
Y __N__ I am able to ask for help when I need it.

If you answered *Yes* to most of the questions, you're a perfect candidate for either. sales or network marketing or real estate or any other endeavor that requires you to follow established routines and work closely with people you don't know. If you answered *No* to most questions, you would probably be happier in another kind of business.

❄ CHAPTER TWENTY-THREE ❄

Stay on Track
While Keeping Your Balance

> *"Our highest need-indeed, what makes us human- was what is*
> *called self-actualization, the yearning to engage our talents and*
> *realize our potential."*
> *–Abraham Maslov*

ACCOUNTABILITY – THE SECRET TOOL

Two of the most important qualities of a successful person are the ability to stay the course, to keep focused on what is important without becoming sidetracked by trivial side issues; and the ability to keep a sense of balance in life between work, family, friends and commitments. The secret tool for achieving both is accountability — the consistent self-evaluation to make certain we're doing what we should be doing at all times.

If you've ever belonged to a book club or initiated a walking program with a friend or joined a weight loss group, you know the power of being accountable for reading the assigned book or showing up for the workouts or facing the scales. We start learning accountability in school when we do homework and take tests. As adults, the tests are subtler but very much there. They take the form of reports given to our supervisor each week, sales projections that must be met each month or income tax forms filed every year. It's all about owning up to what you did during a specific period of time. Accountability is the best way to stay on track with all you have to do

As much as we grumble about having to be accountable, we would live in chaos if suddenly there weren't any checks and balances in our lives. There would be no need to accomplish anything and for some people, that would equal permission to do nothing.

The more accountable you become, to your friends, your mentors, and yourself, the faster you will progress and the easier it will be to see how far you have come and see your progress over time.

BE ACCOUNTABLE TO YOUR FRIENDS/CHAMPIONSHIP CIRCLE

The amazing thing about your vision for your future is that it grows stronger the more you talk about it. If you keep your vision bottled up inside yourself, never telling anyone else what you are planning and working for, it becomes less real, less vibrant, and less attainable. On the other hand, if you describe what you're looking toward in vivid detail, with so much passion that your listeners become just as excited as you, so they can feel it and taste it and touch it as you can — then you're started firmly on the path to achieving it.

Sometimes we're so unsure of our own ability to carry out what we want to do that we are very quiet about it. If no one knows what we're attempting, no one will know when we fail. That's a defeatist attitude that guarantees you won't stay on track. When people understand your goals they unconsciously try to help you. So I'm encouraging you to tell the world what you're going to do.

Working toward turning your vision into a reality is the same story, although perhaps in less dramatic circumstances. If everyone knows you're trying to quit smoking or lose weight or tone up or learn to play guitar or make extra money — whatever it is you want to do — your good friends and your Championship Circle team will encourage you to follow through. If no one knows you've given up chocolate, it's pretty easy to have a piece, but when your vision is common knowledge, you don't want to disappoint your friends by slipping back into old habits.

They may not say anything but there will be that look in their eyes. The opinion of your personal community of friends and family is a strong incentive to stay on track. Use it!

Miriam decided for the umpteenth time to stop smoking. Her friends smoked. Her fiancé smoked. And she really liked smoking — a lot. But she realized it wasn't good for her and the time had come to quit. This time she told everyone she knew about her struggle. She was upfront about how difficult it was and how tempted she remained. Miriam quickly found out who her true friends were. Her fiancé decided to quit too. At social gatherings, the smokers stayed as far away from her as they could. When she said, "Maybe one cigarette wouldn't hurt," people gathered around her and refused to let her succumb until the craving passed.

"I've tried dozens of times on my own," Miriam says, "but I was successful when I let other people share my challenge. I found a real Championship Circle team who helped me change a bad habit — this time for good."

* * * * * * * * * *

John, who is Mormon and a highly respected elder of the church, tells a similar story. When he was in high school, he was as curious about drugs and alcohol as his non-Mormon friends. John hung out with the jocks and often went to school parties. Whenever someone offered him a smoke or a beer, his friends would interfere saying, "He can't have that." Even though they weren't the same religion, they kept him on the right path at a time in his life when he was open to going astray.

It's only fair to repeat the warning I gave you earlier. Sometimes even the best-intentioned people will try to destroy your dream. They don't want to see you fail, but they also don't want you to outshine them and move off into a life they can't envision. If you get static — negative feedback — from those you thought were friends, understand where they're coming from and RUN IN THE OPPOSITE DIRECTION! You can stay in touch in a peripheral way, but you need to surround yourself with a team that applauds and inspires you, not a group that tries to drag you down to their level.

BE ACCOUNTABLE TO YOUR MENTORS

By now I hope you've at least begun to identify and interact with mentors who are helping guide you on the road to success. They will be a strong link in your chain of accountability.

A good mentor will give you goals to reach between meetings. These aren't as big as your Power-Want goals or your Future Book dreams. These are smaller goals that take you another step along the path you must follow.

Every time you meet with your mentor or your Master Mind group, report on your progress and set new goals you want to reach. If you need help, ask for it but don't allow a lack of information to be an excuse to slack off for a week or month. Make the necessary call or find the books or audio and video programs that will bring you up to speed as soon as possible.

Catherine had started with a network marketing company as an independent distributor. She was all fired-up with enthusiasm and determined to beat all the others in her sponsor's organization. When I suggested that she fax me her contact sheet every week so we could talk about her prospects and their responses to her sales pitch, she said she could do it alone. "I'm accustomed to setting goals for myself," she told me. "I'm going to make five calls to prospective customers every evening and 20 calls on Saturday. Wait until next month's meeting. I'll show you."

She had all her Monday calls planned out, but that Monday night she thought she'd better get a proper workspace put together before she started. One day wouldn't make any difference. Tuesday there was a special on cable that she didn't want to miss and probably anyone she could call would be watching the same thing. Wednesday night she had to work late and stopped for dinner on the way home, by which time it was too late to call anyone. Thursday night she had promised to baby-sit for her sister but she would catch up the next evening. On Friday, the office gang went out for pizza after work. Saturday she came down with a cold so, she reasoned, she might as well take the weekend off and start on Monday.

At the next month's meeting, Catherine showed me the list of calls she had made. She hadn't gotten through to the first 10 people yet. "I just kept figuring I could wait one more day," she confessed. "and tomorrow never seemed to come."

Together, we set up a schedule, and she agreed to fax me every day with a list of people she had contacted. The minute the accountability factor kicked in, Catherine became a dynamo. She started doing twice what she expected and indeed became one of my best distributors building a strong and lucrative business. "You can bet I insist my associates are accountable to me," she says. "I learned the hard way that it works."

Unless you are one of those singularly self-disciplined individuals who never gets distracted from the task at hand, you will benefit from being accountable to someone after you have a plan to follow. Most humans want to please others and one way to do that is to keep your word and prove it. A good mentor is a benevolent guide who still makes you toe the mark and motivates you to stay on track by affirming your successes and assessing your failures on a regular basis.

MAINTAINING YOUR MOTIVATION

Now let's talk about what to do when you're almost where you want to be and it feels as if the growth will keep on coming even if you just coast along. In time, that day will arrive, but too often people quit before they have their fingers firmly around the brass ring. Quitting too soon is almost as bad as not getting started. It would be like knitting a sweater and casting off the stitches before the sweater was long enough.

Whether your spirit is flagging because you've run into a rough patch — or because you've encountered some failures — or because you're tired of struggling to get ahead — or the goal looks too far away — then it's time to take a break. That's right, take an hour — or even a day — and allow yourself to stop and regroup. It's always easier to start again from a standing start than to try and change direction when you're in motion.

Sometimes it's necessary to take an R&R day, giving yourself the rest-and-recreation break that will recharge your batteries and let you begin again with new determination. Go out and see a good movie. Treat yourself to a comedy show — or just turn on your cable's comedy or cartoon channel. There's nothing like a good laugh to revive your spirits. Watch reruns of *I Love Lucy, Cheers,* or *Seinfeld.* You will be so much happier and feel so much lighter after enjoying these simple diversions.

Have you ever heard the phrase, "Let go and let God"? Belief in a higher power is the source behind what many people believe gets them through though times. Sometimes we work so hard to achieve small results that we're left exasperated. Perhaps people around us may continually criticize our efforts so we begin to doubt our ability. If this describes you, stop immediately and understand it's quite normal. I've found that after the first euphoria, that heady feeling of new freedom and unlimited opportunity, there comes a time when it's hard to keep yourself excited. In school, we called it "sophomore slump." It's that time when you know what you have to do and are busy doing it, but you seem so far from your goal.

I've watched people sabotage their success. Just when they're on the verge of a breakthrough, success is in sight, they unconsciously set themselves up to fail, making a decision that stops their momentum. They fear success and the changes it may bring or deep down inside their low self-esteem and negative self-talk takes over and they believe they just don't deserve success.

This is one of the most dangerous times for any entrepreneur. If you lose your focus now, it will be very difficult to get enthused all over again. It's the time when you want to revisit your Future Book more often. Read your list of Power-Wants aloud at least once a day. If one of your Power-Wants is to drive a Mercedes, go to your local dealership and take one for a test drive. If you want a new house in an upscale neighborhood, have a realtor show you what's available. Do everything you can to make your dreams and goals real, something you can taste and touch and feel. That's often enough to switch your motor back on high.

BE ACCOUNTABLE TO YOURSELF

In the final analysis, the one person on the planet you must be accountable to is yourself. Though I firmly believe you also have to be accountable to others, and in the process you will gain the skills to strengthen your own resolve. No matter how many times you have to check in with someone else, you are still alone a great deal of the time.

As you become comfortable with telling someone else about your challenges and victories, you'll soon become more adept at being your own judge and jury.

If you say you listened to a tape or read a chapter in a book or went to a meeting in another part of town, your mentor may not be able to verify whether you're being totally truthful — but you know. If you say you made those dreaded cold calls everyone hates but never actually picked up the phone, you may be able to fake it to your sponsor but you can't lie to yourself.

It's said, "You are what you do when no one else is looking," and that's the kind of personal accountability we all must strive for.

PROVIDING FOR BALANCE

Only you know what is necessary for you to stay centered and feeling good physically and psychologically. In general, we all need relaxation of some sort every day. It can be as simply as 15 minutes soaking in a bubble bath or half an hour on the back porch with a glass of lemonade and a good book. You might benefit from a ten-minute meditation, allowing yourself to escape from constant yammering of television, radio and kids or a walk around the block. Whatever it takes for you to recharge your batteries, schedule the time to do it. Write it down in your appointment book and treat this time like any other commitment.

In Chapter 24 I'll talk more about how to achieve balance as you plan to step back and reassess your new life, preparing to make new changes or improvements or leave it behind and tackle another challenge. The exit strategy is a vital part of any business plan, and you'll learn how to work toward yours in the following pages.

How to Stay Accountable

In the resource section, I've suggested some books and tapes that will help you not only be accountable, but also assist you in doing some of the tasks none of us really likes, like those pesky cold calls. Be sure to keep a small notebook in which you can track your daily to do list, prioritizing the items at the beginning of each day and evaluating how well you've done at the end of each day. When you write down these tasks you'll reduce your stress level. No longer will you have to try to remember everything, and you won't find things slipping through the cracks because you forgot. At the end of the week, it'll be like spring cleaning. You'll have cleared your head of clutter, and you'll feel a sense of accomplishment as you look at all that you have done. This notebook is another great place to keep a picture of your "Why."

Instead of a typical exercise in this chapter, I've given you an accountability report form. You can use it as a template to draw up your own form or you can duplicate several blank copies and use them. Each form is good for four weeks. Using this with my network marketing group I was able to build one of the largest, most successful network of distributorships in a remarkably short period of time. You might want to make revisions in the specific commitments to conform to the activities that lead you toward your goal.

Suggested Resources:

Books:

Cold Calling for Women: Opening Doors and Closing Sales by Wendy Weiss. (DFD Publishing: 2000 — ISBN: 0-9671-2680-0)

I Could Do Anything If I Knew What It Was: How to Discover What You Really Want and How to Get It by Barbara Sher (Delacorte Press:1994 — ISBN: 0-385-307788-8)

100 Ways to Motivate Yourself: Change Your Life Forever by Steve Chandler (Career Press, 1996 — ISBN # 1-56414-249-3)Call 1-800-CAREER-1

To Build the Life You Want, Create the Work You Love: The Spiritual Dimension of Entrepreneuring by Marsha Sinetar (St. Martin's Press: 1996 — ISBN: 0-3121-4141-6)

Take It From Me: Life's a Struggle But You Can Win by Erin Brockovich, Marc Eliot.(McGraw-Hill//Contemporary Books: 2001 — ISBN: 0-0713-8379-4)

Never Say Never: 10 Lessons to Turn You Can't Into Yes I Can by Phyllis George, Rick Pitino (McGraw-Hill/Contemporary Books: 2002 — ISBN: 0-0714-0878-9)

Feel the Fear and Do It Anyway by Susan Jeffers, Ph.D. (Fawcett Book, Ballantine Publishing, 1987 — ISDN: 0-449-90292-7)

Movie:

Erin Brockovich starring Julia Roberts, Albert Finney. Universal/MCA. VHS, DVD.

GIMME FIVE! EXERCISE #23

My Monthly Accountability Report
Developing My Championship Circle

Name:_____Month: _____

My "Why": _____

My Weekly Goal: _____

My Monthly Goal: _____

My Commitments	Week 1	Week 2	Week 3	Week 4
	Goal — Results			

I will call people: _____   _____   _____   _____
(use FORMula to build bridges, find peole who are open to joining a
    Championship Team)

I will do follow-up calls: _____   _____   _____   _____
(continue to call if unavailable)

I will read book chapters,
or listen to audiotapes/CDs,
or watch programs to develop
my knowledge, attitude, and skills: _____   _____   _____   _____

I will attend meetings to meet
new people (social parties, business
functions, community gatherings):   _____   _____   _____   _____

I will spend in leisure pursuits: _____   _____   _____   _____

Totals: _____   _____   _____   _____

"Today I'll do what others won't, so tomorrow I'll have what others don't."

❧ CHAPTER TWENTY-FOUR ❧

Every Plan Has an Exit Strategy

> *"You've got to know when to hold them,*
> *know when to fold them."*
> *–Kenny Rogers*

DO YOU NEED TO STICK THINGS OUT?

That's what we were taught in school and by our parents. "Don't quit. Stick it out. It will get better." In truth, sometimes it won't. Sometimes the situation isn't going to improve. Sometimes you're ready to leave and do something else. It can be a bad situation you're leaving or a better one you're going toward, but either way the fact is sometimes you're better off changing your position and doing something else.

In life, just like in a card game, you have to know when it's time to fold your cards, say thank you and get up from the table because for you the game is over.

When you've got money in the bank, income producing properties or passive residual income flowing in, your original Power-Wants achieved and your Future Book now your reality, then it's time to start thinking of how you're going to stop jumping the hurdles, get off the horse and sit in the shade for awhile. It may happen before all your dreams are realized, but it will feel best if you wait until you're totally comfortable before you leave the hunt.

If all is going according to plan, that change might mean you're ready to ease up and kick back because you've achieved your major goals. You no longer need or want to work as hard as you did in the beginning. It's time to smell those roses you've been cultivating for so long.

> Jon and his wife run a consulting business in California. Initially working out of their home, they knew they were successful when they were signing the lease for the new office and growing their staff to thirty people. They were making really good money now and had a clientele list and reputation anyone would be proud of. The business was big and the problems were bigger: paperwork, employee issues, procedure changes and talk about stress. Jon and his wife found they were no longer enjoying their work and decided success meant downsizing for them. Gone were all but a select few clients, no more employees and hassles. Jon and his wife were back to working out of their home and enjoying their work.

If you aren't yet where you want to be but the people you're working with lack your dedication and zeal, maybe it's time to find a new set of people. If your Championship Circle isn't helping you, they're hindering you. It's a very black-and-white issue, no shades of gray. If they are hindering, it's time to replace them, difficult as it might be. These are choices you have to make. No one can make them for you. You must be aware of what's going on around you, consistently evaluate your progress and be ready to call it quits rather than watch your plans and dreams falter.

WATCH FOR THE EXIT SIGNS

In any business endeavor there are exit signs, very similar to those on the highways in that they usually point to a new and potentially exciting destination. I have turned off some very promising roads when the going started to get bumpy, and I realized potholes were right around the curve.

> In 1981, I worked for Digital Equipment Corporation (DEC). I invested in the employee stock option plan. My stockbroker at the time told me it was a very stable stock holding at around $80/share. My stock, which was all purchased at a discount through the company program, grew and split twice. I sold it and left the company when the stock was over $100 per share.
>
> DEC was a company that had grown 10-30% a year for over 30 years before suddenly losing its competitive edge when SUN Microsystems came into the market. SUN offered smaller, cheaper, faster computers that had an

open architecture allowing others to write software programs to run on it. Had I continued to hold that DEC stock, like so many who played the stock game, I would have been down 90% instead of making a nice profit.

If I had remained an employee of DEC as so many other did, I would have eventually lost my job or been absorbed by another company. In which I would have had to prove my worth to management yet again. What I did have was a long-standing exit strategy I could put into action — and it worked.

An exit strategy has saved me more than once in my career. When the network marketing company I devoted my life to for several years fell victim to market changes, I didn't stick around to go down with the ship. With poor management decisions, product delivery issues, servicing issues, personnel changes — and even misuse of the capital they did have — the burden to increase sales fell on the reps without the comfortable payouts we had in the past. Again, I got out before the boom was lowered and was fairly unscathed, unlike some who refused to see the handwriting on the wall.

Whenever you work for other people, you have no control over how the company is run or what provisions are being made for problems in the marketplace that will affect your future. If you must work for someone else for a time, keep your eyes and ears open. Don't let yourself become complacent, assuming the good times will continue forever. Remember Enron. Remember Arthur Anderson. Remember WorldCom and Global Crossing. The rank-and-file, those who weren't in top management, were crushed by the so-called leaders they supported.

Jim has a tremendous background with a large international organization. He has achieved success in every endeavor of his life, both starting and building businesses and in his personal life. One of his greatest attributes is his ability to focus and move forward through any and all adversity.

As I started to question the direction of a company for which we were both independent reps, I scaled back my participation to see what changes management would make in the product offerings, service, support and compensation structure. I had watched this company fumble one decision after another, eventually destroying the confidence and morale of its top leadership because we couldn't sustain our business or clients. Unfortunately, the company failed to communicate with its leaders. They felt we were dispensable, and all they'd have to do is go out and create new leaders.

I put my business on hold, but Jim remained with the company four years longer, building and losing four separate teams of distributors. He was loyal to the founders and their vision, completely focused on the original goals.He remained focused to a fault, spending more and more time and money trying to save his business. Eventually he saw that there was no recovery and he too left — with nothing.

Jim has moved on and is successfully building another company. He'll always be able to make money. It's his time that he won't ever be able to recover.

THE JOSIE RULE

After many years of watching one corporate disaster after another and trying to patch up the shattered egos of friends who were caught in the vise because they were afraid to forego "security" for the unknown, my rule is:

If it's happened before, it will happen again.

Don't let it happen to you!

No one is immune from bad judgment. Throughout this book I've quoted from and recommended Napoleon Hill's classic book, *Think and Grow Rich,* which he wrote over 20 years while working for the steel magnate, Andrew Carnegie. After he interviewed 500 millionaires, he came up with the common denominators for success. It's a gem of a book, powerful pages of advice you can buy for $5.95 — and it's also a lesson for all of us.

Napoleon Hill himself was never a financial success. He always worked for other people. After Andrew Carnegie died, the Chicago insurance magnate, W. Clement Stone, hired him, wrote books with him, and supported him until Hill died in 1970. For all his writing about how to grow rich, Napoleon Hill never followed his own advice. He never broke free of the shackles of working for someone else to become self-employed and control his own destiny. He never benefited from the residual income that would have been the inevitable result of the several books he wrote and lectures he gave.

However, thanks to his book, which has sold over seven million copies, the same thing doesn't have to happen to you. Successful people are always open to learning, wanting to become better people who exert a positive influence those around them.

How to Plan an Exit Strategy

Whatever you do, whatever situation you're in, don't jump off the cliff until you're certain you have a place to land. No matter how ready you are to retire or to change occupations or to quit your job and start your own company, be patient until you're sure you can support yourself in your new endeavor.

> Janet decided she couldn't stand another day of her job. Every day was drudgery, and of course, the more she thought of it as drudgery, the worse it became. Finally she was getting sick on Sunday nights just thinking about work the next morning. So on the day she turned 62, she gave her notice and signed up for her much-diminished social security. She had a small pension from her late husband so there wasn't a lot of money. The social security rules prohibited her from making much without losing her benefits.
>
> Worst of all, Janet had made no plans for what to do with her days. Her children lived across the country. Her income didn't allow for many trips or even long phone calls. Her friends were all still working. It didn't take long before she got very tired of daytime television and she felt too young to join the senior center.
>
> "If I had only thought it out more fully, I would have figured out some way to make the job more interesting or to start something else. Instead, I jumped without a safety net. I'll never do that again," she says. Today she's trying to find ways she can be useful to her community and still make some money under the social security guidelines. "I try to stay optimistic but I'm angriest at me because I did this to myself," Janet says.

Janet is by no means an unusual case. Young people often make the same mistake. They quit a job or change a behavior or drive toward a goal without giving a single thought to what will replace it. They figure they will find something, land on their feet somehow. Once upon a time in another century maybe, but in the new millennium one cannot count on that happening.

Just as you've planned your steps to take in order to attain your Power-Wants and fulfill the promise of your Future Book, think carefully about the decision to leave. As you plan your exit strategy, you should:

- Write out the steps you have to take before you leave one activity for another.

- Talk to your mentors and the members of your Championship Circle. See if they agree with your evaluation of your situation. Sometimes a fresh viewpoint can make the unbearable able to be tolerated for a bit longer.
- Ask yourself what else is going on in your life that may be affecting how you feel.
- Determine what the future will hold if you quit and do nothing — or go into a new endeavor.
- Make lists of the pros and cons of staying — and exiting.
- Be very specific about how much money you will have to live on and what you will do to fill your days.
- Consider how your actions will affect your family. If you're not married, how will this affect your relationship with a significant other?
- Set a timetable for your exit and be prepared to alter it as conditions change.

The timetable is a critical part of the exit strategy process. You want to put this plan into effect at the best time for you, which may or may not be the best time for others to lose your input. Every situation is different, but usually it's best to take your time. Prepare yourself and others for the changes that will happen when you leave the day-to-day operation. Often it makes more sense to ease out gradually, being certain those you leave behind will be able to continue the operation and keep your residual income flowing. If you own real estate as income property, you will want to assure yourself that your managers are competent and in control. If it's a network marketing group, your top producing representatives need to be ready to step into your shoes and continue training and support so the residuals keep coming and the group doesn't lose momentum. If you're relying on a stock portfolio, you want to have a broker who's watching out for your interests so if you're in the Bahamas when a buy or sell order has to be placed, they will contact you and operate in your best interests.

However it works out for you, put the dates down in your calendar and ease yourself and your associates into your new and exciting life.

PLOTTING THE EXIT STRATEGY ON PAPER

By now you know I like to write things down. It's the only way you'll keep your focus and meet your goals. The same rule holds for the exit strategy. In Exercise #24 you will begin the monthly review process so you know when it's time to leave.

Suggested Resources:

Books:

Work Less, Make More: Stop Working So Hard and Create the Life You Really Want! by Jennifer White (John Wiley & Sons:1999 — ISBN: 0471354856)

Breathing Space: Living and Working at a Comfortable Space in a Sped Up Society by Jeff Davidson. (Breathing Space Institute: 2000 — ISBN: 0942361326)

Life Matters: Creating a Dynamic Balance of Work, Family, Time & Money by A. Roger Merrill, Rebecca Merrill. (McGraw-Hill Trade: 2003 — ISBN: 0071422137)

Take Time for Your Life: A Personal Coach's Seven-Step Program for Creating the Life You Want by Cheryl Richardson. (Broadway Books:1999 — ISBN: 0767902076)

Movie:

Life is Beautiful, 1998 starring Roberto Benigni, Nicoletta Brashchi and Giorgio Cantarini. A unforgettable fable that proves love, family and imagination conquer all.

Songs:

Simply the Best, sung by Tina Turner
Respect, sung by Aretha Franklin

GIMME FIVE! – EXERCISE #24

Evaluate your career, your investments, and your business by reviewing the following questions each and every month until you feel you are on track and progressing toward your goal then continue to review the quarterly.

My Exit Strategy Worksheet

I am actively pursuing my goal to: _____

_____

I have given myself (time) to accomplish this goal. _____

_____

I am on track to reaching my goal because (use quantitative measures or milestones, i.e. I have taken two classes and achieved a 3.0 average, I have increased my salary by 5% or my investments have grown by 10%) ____

_____

_____

_____

I have not reached my goal because: _____

_____

_____

_____

_____

In order to reach my goal, I will have to: _____

_____

_____

_____

_____

I will contact these people and / or resort to these resources and conduct the following activities in an effort to continue moving toward my goal:____

_____

_____

_____

If I do not reach my goal by (date), I will evaluate what I can do to achieve my goal. If I do not think I can attain my goal, or if my priorities or circumstances have changed, then I know it is time to exit from this strategy.

_____

_____

⚜ CHAPTER TWENTY-FIVE ⚜

Time to Review

> *"A woman's life can really be a succession of lives, each revolving around some emotionally compelling situation or challenge, and each marked off by some intense experience."*
> —Wallis Simpson, Duchess of Windsor

LOOKING BACK

Until now, everything we've talked about relates to the "here and now" and the results you'll see in the near future. While you're probably reading this before the *Gimme Five!* Method has paid off for you, I want you to come back to it in five years and read it again. By then this book should be pretty dog-eared, tattered and torn. You can no longer plead ignorance. If you've done the work I've asked to you do in this book, you've been exposed to who you are and what you consider your Power-Wants. The *Gimme Five!* Method has given you a way to set goals, sharpen your skills, and build a team to propel and support you in making your Future Book a reality and not a dream.

Life is short and for those who approach it with enthusiasm, vision, and courage it's much too short. Make your decision today to attain the life you deserve — and renew that decision everyday hereafter. You've read through many stories of lives transformed. You realize that life is an exciting game if you're in the thick of the action and you're not content to sit watching from the sidelines. Every day is the first day of the rest of your life. Don't waste a precious minute of it.

The five basic rules of the *Gimme Five!* Method are simple and deceptively powerful.

To make them most effective in your life, copy them and post them where you'll see them every day. Read them aloud. Let them become part of your subconscious Reticular Activating System so that they guide your behavior the way an operating system guides the way a computer runs.

When you have fully assimilated these rules, the positive changes in your life will continue to propel you toward success.

Gimme Five! Rule Number One
Become Self-Smart
"Know who you are and never allow anyone else to define your life."

Gimme Five! Rule Number Two:
Become Vision- and Goal-Smart
"You are who you think you are —
but you will be who you believe you will be."

Gimme Five! Rule Number Three:
Become Money-Smart
"Use money as a tool instead of a prize and it will build you a fortune."

Gimme Five! Rule Number Four:
Become People-Smart
"The more you understand people, the more successful you will be."

Gimme Five! Rule Number Five:
Become Options-Smart
"You have only one option — the option to do something now."

In the final exercises, I want you to look back over the past five years. That's right. Don't do it now. Wait until you've worked the _Gimme Five!_ Method for five years and then come back and look at where you were and how far you've come. When you fill out exercise 25-A, compare it with the same form you filled out so many months ago in the first chapter. And then go to exercise 25-B and answer some basic questions about your journey. This is a when you keep yourself motivated with new visions, new goals, and new dreams.

ONE LAST JOSIE RULE:
Give yourself a high five!

That's right — reward yourself for a job well done. That's the whole point of _Gimme Five!_ It's positive reinforcement. We need to celebrate every victory, no matter how small and remind ourselves how far we've come and how hard we've worked to get here.

Whether you're reading this when you're just starting — or five years down the road — I say "Congratulations!" You've embarked on a life-long journey that will be the most rewarding change you've ever made. "_Gimme Five!_"

SUCCESS TECHNIQUE #5:

Conduct a personal annual review. Give yourself a score between 1 (worst) and 5 (best) for how well you've done throughout the year in becoming a Gimme Five! _"SMART" expert. Be brutally honest about how hard and how well you have learned your new life skills — and don't forget to generously praise yourself on your efforts._

GIMME FIVE! EXERCISE #25A

Where do you live? *(House? Apartment? City? Rural area?)* _____

_____

What is your family like? *(Alone? Married? Children? Ages?)*_____

_____

What type of work do you do? *(Career? Self-employed? Homemaker?)*_____

_____

_____

Who do you hang out with? *(Friends? Family? Co-workers? Loner?)* _____

_____

_____

_____

_____

What have you accomplished? *(Children? Work? Community? Church?)* _____

_____

_____

_____

_____

What is your health situation? *(Medical problems? Overweight? Stressed?)* ___

_____

_____

What is your financial situation? *(Struggling? Comfortable? Bleak?)* _____

_____

_____

What part does spirituality play in your life?_____

_____

_____

What is your lifestyle? *(Single? Working wife/mother? Single mother? Student?)*

_____

_____

_____

What is your happiness quotient? *(On scale of 1-10 where 1 is miserable and 10 is terrific.)* _____

GIMME FIVE! EXERCISE #25B

How has my life changed since I started the *Gimme Five!* Method? _____

_____

_____

_____

_____

Which of my dreams are now realities? _____

_____

_____

_____

What are the most positive changes I've made? _____

_____

_____

_____

Knowing what I now know, what would I have done differently? _____

_____

_____

_____

How has my Championship Circle changed? _____

_____

_____

_____

Do I still work with my mentors — and am I now mentoring others? _____

_____

_____

_____

What new Power-Wants are in my Future Book? _____

_____

_____

_____

What deadline have I put on achieving these goals? _____

_____

_____

_____

If it's to be, it's up to me!

Note from Josie Melo

The *Gimme Five!* Method has transformed my life and the lives of many others. I congratulate, applaud and respect you for your courage and tenacity to make your life the best you can, making the decision to change and taking the actions for the lifestyle you desire.

I am exceedingly grateful for all the success, love and blessings in my life: family, friends, stability, security, work that fulfills me and freedom. I look forward to meeting, encouraging and helping more people achieve their goals through the *Gimme Five!* Method and look forward to the day when other *Gimme Five!* Method certified trainers (details on my website: www.gimmefivemethod.com) can conduct mini-workshops around the country and in other countries transforming people, feeding them knowledge and supporting their efforts to live a life they deserve.

I would like to hear from you at any time while you're working through the *Gimme Five!* Method. Let me know your challenges and your victories. I want to know how the process is working for you, what specific tools or actions are you taking, what results have you experienced and with your permission use your story to help encourage, motivate and build the confidence of others.

You can reach me at my website: www.GimmeFiveMethod.com or write me at Freedom to Succeed Seminars, P.O. Box 3160, Los Altos, CA 94024.

• Notes •

• Notes •

Quick Order Form

Book Price: $14.95 US / $21.95 CDN
Sales Tax: California Residents ONLY add 8.25%
Postage and handling: $4.95 for first book, $1.00 for each additional book

Telephone Orders: Call toll free 1-888-748-9088
Fax orders (send this form): USA 1-650-210-9088

Online orders: www.gimmefivemethod.com

Mail orders (send this form):
Freedom to Succeed
P.O. Box 3160, Los Altos, CA 94024

I understand that I have a 30-day, 100% refund guarantee on any returned item.

Name: _____

Address: _____

City:_____State:_____ Zip _____

Telephone:*_____

Email address: _____

Payment: Money Order   Amex   Discover   Visa   MC

Please Print Clearly

Name on Card: _____

Card Number:_____Exp. Date: _____

Signature: _____
*Required for credit card orders. Your contact information will not be shared with
   other businesses or organizations.

(This form is for orders within the Continental U.S. only)
Please visit www.gimmefivemethod.com
for information on shipping orders outside the U.S. and
volume or reseller orders.